KB043834

Reading Schedule

이 책은 총 32,000여개의 단어로 구성되어 있습니다.(중복 포함, 1페이지는 대략 171단어)
분당 150단어 읽기는 원어민이 말하는 속도입니다. 먼저 이 기준을 목표로 시작해보세요.

● 1회 읽기

날 짜	/	/	/	/	/
시 간	~	~	~	~	~
페이지	~	~	~	~	~

내용 이해도   ✓ 90%이상   ✓ 70%   ✓ 50%   ✓ 30%이하

리딩속도 계산   214 ÷ ☐ × 154 = ☐
전체 페이지   시간(분)   1페이지 당 평균 단어수   분당 읽은 단어수

● 2회 읽기

날 짜	/	/	/	/	/
시 간	~	~	~	~	~
페이지	~	~	~	~	~

내용 이해도   ✓ 90%이상   ✓ 70%   ✓ 50%   ✓ 30%이하

리딩속도 계산   214 ÷ ☐ × 154 = ☐
전체 페이지   시간(분)   1페이지 당 평균 단어수   분당 읽은 단어수

● 3회 읽기

날 짜	/	/	/	/	/
시 간	~	~	~	~	~
페이지	~	~	~	~	~

내용 이해도   ✓ 90%이상   ✓ 70%   ✓ 50%   ✓ 30%이하

리딩속도 계산   214 ÷ ☐ × 154 = ☐
전체 페이지   시간(분)   1페이지 당 평균 단어수   분당 읽은 단어수

식은 죽
먹기야~

● 전체 평가

체감 난이도 ☑ 상　　☑ 상중　☑ 중　　☑ 중하　☑ 하

읽기 만족도 ☑ 나는 리딩의 고수!

☑ 좀 잘했군요~

☑ 노력하세요.

☑ 난 머리가 안 좋나봐 -.-;

사람은 무엇으로 사는가

리딩 속도가 빨라지는 영어책 015

사람은 무엇으로 사는가
WHAT MEN LIVE BY AND OTHER TALES

2020년 10월 10일 초판 1쇄 인쇄
2020년 10월 15일 초판 1쇄 발행

지은이 톨스토이
발행인 손건
편집기획 김상배
마케팅 이언영
디자인 이성세
제작 최승용
인쇄 선경프린테크

발행처 LanCom 랭컴
주소 서울시 금천구 시흥대로193, 709호
등록번호 제 312-2006-00060호
전화 02) 2636-0895
팩스 02) 2636-0896
홈페이지 www.lancom.co.kr

ISBN 979-11-89204-72-3 13740

사람은 무엇으로 사는가

WHAT MEN LIVE BY
AND OTHER TALES

톨스토이 지음

LanCom
Language & Communication

CONTENTS

사람은 무엇으로 사는가 −7

1 −11   **2** −15   **3** −20   **4** −27

5 −33   **6** −36   **7** −43   **8** −48

9 −53   **10** −57   **11** −62   **12** −67

세 가지 질문 −71

사람에겐 얼마만큼의 땅이 필요한가? −83

1 −84   **2** −88   **3** −93   **4** −99

5 −105   **6** −109   **7** −113   **8** −116

9 −122

바보 이반 −127

1 −128   **2** −132   **3** −138   **4** −142

5 −150   **6** −155   **7** −159   **8** −166

9 −170   **10** −174   **11** −182   **12** −189

에멜리안과 빈 북 −201

사람은 무엇으로 사는가

WHAT MEN LIVE BY

A shoemaker named Simon, who had neither house nor land of his own, lived with his wife and children in a peasant's hut, and earned his living by his work. Work was cheap, but bread was dear, and what he earned he spent for food.

제화공, 구두 만드는 사람 / ~라는 이름의 / (둘 중) 어느 것도 …아니다 / 집 / 땅 / 소유의, 자신의 / 아내, 부인 / 아이들, 어린이들 / 소작농, 소농 / 오두막 / 벌다 / 일, 직장, 직업 / (값이) 싼 / 비싼, 돈이 많이 드는 / 벌다 / …에 (돈을) 쓰다

The man and his wife had but one sheepskin coat between them for winter wear, and even that was torn to tatters, and this was the second year he had been wanting to buy sheep-skins for a new coat.

양가죽 / ~사이에, …간에 / 동복, 겨울옷 / ~조차, 심지어 / 찢어지다, 뜯어지다 / 낡은[해진] 옷, 누더기 / 사다

Before winter Simon saved up a little money: a three-rouble note lay hidden in his wife's box,

~전에, ~에 앞서 / (무엇을 사기 위해) (돈을) 모으다, 저축하다 / 지폐 / 숨기다, 감추다

8

and five roubles and twenty kopeks were owed
루블(러시아 화폐단위) · 코펙(러시아의 화폐 단위, 1/100 ruble)
him by customers in the village.
손님, 고객 · (시골) 마을, 부락, 촌락

So one morning he prepared to go to the vil-
준비하다[시키다]
lage to buy the sheep-skins. He put on over his
사다 · 양가죽 · 입다 · ~위에
shirt his wife's wadded nankeen jacket, and over
셔츠 · 솜을 넣은 · 무명 · 재킷, 웃옷
that he put his own cloth coat.
옷감, 직물, 천

He took the three-rouble note in his pocket,
3루블 · 지폐 · 주머니
cut himself a stick to serve as a staff, and started
자르다 · 막대기 · 지팡이 · ~으로 출발하다
off after breakfast.
아침식사

"I'll collect the five roubles that are due to
모으다, 수집하다(=gather) · ~할 예정이다
me," thought he, "add the three I have got, and
생각하다 · 더하다
that will be enough to buy sheep-skins for the
충분한 · 사다, 구입하다
winter coat."
겨울 외투[코트]

He came to the village and called at a peas-
…에 들르다.
ant's hut, but the man was not at home. The
오두막
peasant's wife promised that the money should
약속하다 · 돈
be paid next week, but she would not pay it
지불하다 · 다음 주
herself. Then Simon called on another peasant,
방문하다(= visit.) · 다른, 다른 사람[것]
but this one swore he had no money, and would
(자기 말이 진실임을) 맹세하다
only pay twenty kopeks which he owed for a
pair of boots Simon had mended.
장화, 부츠 · 수리하다, 고치다

Simon then tried to buy the sheep-skins on
~하려고 시도하다
credit, but the dealer would not trust him.
외상으로, 신용 대출로   (특정 상품을 사고파는) 딜러[중개인]

"Bring your money," said he, "then you may
가져오다
have your pick of the skins. We know what
고르다, 선택하다, 뽑다   알다
debt-collecting is like."
채권 회수, 빚을 거둬들임

So all the business the shoemaker did was to
일, 실적   구두 제조자
get the twenty kopeks for boots he had mended,
20   고치다, 수리하다
and to take a pair of felt boots a peasant gave
펠트(모직이나 털을 압축해서 만든 두꺼운 천)
him to sole with leather.
(신발)밑창을 갈다 (무두질을 거친) 가죽

Simon felt downhearted. He spent the twen-
낙담한, 실망한   쓰다, 소비하다
ty kopeks on vodka, and started homewards
보드카   집 쪽으로, 집을 향하여
without having bought any skins.
~없이

In the morning he had felt the frost; but
서리, 성에
now, after drinking the vodka, he felt warm,
마시다   따뜻한
even without a sheep-skin coat.
~도, 조차, 심지어
He trudged along, striking his stick on the
(지쳐서) 터덜터덜 걷다   (손이나 무기로) 때리다[치다]
frozen earth with one hand, swinging the felt
얼어붙은, 결빙된   (전후좌우로) 흔들리다[흔들다]
boots with the other, and talking to himself.
장화   혼잣말을 하다

1

"I'm quite warm," said he, "though I have
꽤, 상당히, 아주　　　　　　(비록) …이긴 하지만[…인데도]
no sheep-skin coat. I've had a drop, and it
소량, 조금
runs through all my veins.
달리다, 흐르다　　　　정맥, 혈관

"I need no sheep-skins. I go along and don't
필요한
worry about anything. That's the sort of man I
걱정하다　　　　　　　　　종류, 부류, 유형 (=kind)
am! What do I care? I can live without sheep-
상관하다, 신경 쓰다
skins. I don't need them.

"My wife will fret, to be sure. And, true
조바심치다, 조마조마하다　　　사실인, 참인
enough, it is a shame; one works all day long,
수치심, 창피　　　　일하다
and then does not get paid.

"Stop a bit! If you don't bring that money
조금, 다소, 약간　　　　가져오다
along, sure enough I'll skin you, blessed if I
확실히 ~을 할　　　　가죽을 벗기다　(신의) 가호를 빌다
don't. How's that?

"He pays twenty kopeks at a time! What can I do with twenty kopeks? Drink it-that's all one can do! Hard up, he says he is! So he may be--but what about me? You have a house, and cattle, and everything; I've only what I stand up in! You have corn of your own growing; I have to buy every grain. Do what I will, I must spend three roubles every week for bread alone. I come home and find the bread all used up, and I have to fork out another rouble and a half. So just pay up what you owe, and no nonsense about it!"

By this time he had nearly reached the shrine at the bend of the road. Looking up, he saw something whitish behind the shrine.

The daylight was fading, and the shoemaker peered at the thing without being able to make out what it was.

"There was no white stone here before. Can it be an ox? It's not like an ox. It has a head like a man, but it's too white; and what could a man be doing there?"

12

He came closer, so that it was clearly visible.
더 가까이 / 똑똑히 보이는.

To his surprise it really was a man, alive or dead,
놀랍게도 / 정말로, 진짜로 / 살아있는 / 죽은

sitting naked, leaning motionless against the shrine.
벌거벗은, 아무것도 걸치지 않은 / 움직이지 않는

Terror seized the shoemaker, and he thought, "Some one has killed him, stripped him, and left him there. If I meddle I shall surely get into trouble."
공포, 두려움 / 꽉 붙잡다, 사로잡다 / 죽이다 / 옷을 벗기다 / 간섭하다[참견하다/끼어들다] (=interfere) / 곤란에 부딪치다, 곤경에 빠지다, 큰일나다

So the shoemaker went on. He passed in front of the shrine so that he could not see the man. When he had gone some way, he looked back, and saw that the man was no longer leaning against the shrine, but was moving as if looking towards him.
지나가다 / ~앞 / 성소, 제단 / 돌아보다 / 더 이상 ~ 아니다 / 움직이다 / (~을) 향하여

The shoemaker felt more frightened than before, and thought, "Shall I go back to him, or shall I go on? If I go near him something dreadful may happen. Who knows who the fellow is? He has not come here for any good. If I go near him he may jump up and throttle me, and there will be no getting away. Or if not, he'd
더욱 / 겁먹은, 무서워하는 / 가까이, 근처에 / 끔찍한, 지독한 / 녀석, 친구 / 목을 졸라 죽이다

still be a burden on one's hands. What could I do with a naked man? I couldn't give him my last clothes. Heaven only help me to get away!"

So the shoemaker hurried on, leaving the shrine behind him-when suddenly his conscience smote him, and he stopped in the road.

"What are you doing, Simon?" said he to himself. "The man may be dying of want, and you slip past afraid. Have you grown so rich as to be afraid of robbers? Ah, Simon, shame on you!"

So he turned back and went up to the man.

2

Simon approached the stranger, looked at
다가가다, 접근하다   낯선[모르는] 사람
him, and saw that he was a young man,
젊은
fit, with no bruises on his body, only evidently
(몸이) 건강한   멍   몸, 신체, 육체   분명히, 눈에 띄게
freezing and frightened, and he sat there leaning
얼어붙은   겁 먹은, 두려워하는   ~에 기대다
back without looking up at Simon, as if too faint
마치 ~인 것처럼   실신할 것 같은
to lift his eyes.
들어올리다

    Simon went close to him, and then the
가까이
man seemed to wake up. Turning his head,
정신을 차리다
he opened his eyes and looked into Simon's
face. That one look was enough to make Simon
충분한
fond of the man. He threw the felt boots on the
~을 좋아하다[사랑하다]   던지다
ground, undid his sash, laid it on the boots, and
땅바닥   (몸에 두르는) 띠
took off his cloth coat.
벗다

"It's not a time for talking," said he. "Come, put this coat on at once!"

And Simon took the man by the elbows and helped him to rise. As he stood there, Simon saw that his body was clean and in good condition, his hands and feet shapely, and his face good and kind.

He threw his coat over the man's shoulders, but the latter could not find the sleeves. Simon guided his arms into them, and drawing the coat well on, wrapped it closely about him, tying the sash round the man's waist.

Simon even took off his torn cap to put it on the man's head, but then his own head felt cold, and he thought: "I'm quite bald, while he has long curly hair."

So he put his cap on his own head again.

"It will be better to give him something for his feet," thought he; and he made the man sit down, and helped him to put on the felt boots, saying:

"There, friend, now move about and warm
yourself. Other matters can be settled later on.
Can you walk?"

The man stood up and looked kindly at Simon, but could not say a word.

"Why don't you speak?" said Simon. "It's
too cold to stay here, we must be getting home.
There now, take my stick, and if you're feeling
weak, lean on that. Now step out!"

The man started walking, and moved easily,
not lagging behind.

As they went along, Simon asked him, "And
where do you belong to?"

"I'm not from these parts."

"I thought as much. I know the folks here-
abouts. But, how did you come to be there by
the shrine?"

"I cannot tell."

"Has some one been ill-treating you?"

"No one has ill-treated me. God has
punished me."

17

"Of course God rules all. Still, you'll have to find food and shelter somewhere. Where do you want to go to?"

"It is all the same to me."

Simon was amazed. The man did not look like a rogue, and he spoke gently, but yet he gave no account of himself. Still Simon thought, "Who knows what may have happened?" And he said to the stranger:

"Well then, come home with me, and at least warm yourself awhile."

So Simon walked towards his home, and the stranger kept up with him, walking at his side. The wind had risen and Simon felt it cold under his shirt.

He was getting over his tipsiness by now, and began to feel the frost. He went along sniffling and wrapping his wife's coat round him, and he thought to himself:

"There now talk about sheep-skins! I went out for sheep-skins and come home without even a coat to my back, and what is more, I'm

bringing a naked man along with me. Matryona
데려오다, 가져오다 벌거벗은
won't be pleased!"
기쁘게 하다, 즐겁게 하다
And when he thought of his wife he felt
아내, 부인
sad; but when he looked at the stranger and
슬픈   쳐다보다
remembered how he had looked up at him at
기억하다, 생각나다
the shrine, his heart was glad.
성소, 사당   마음   기쁜, 반가운

3

Simon's wife had everything ready early that
day. She had cut wood, brought water, fed
모든 것   일찍
the children, eaten her own meal, and now she
나무   물을 길어오다   먹이다
sat thinking.
끼니, 식사

She wondered when she ought to make
마땅히 ~해야 하다
bread: now or tomorrow? There was still a large
빵   커다란, 큰
piece left.
남은
"If Simon has had some dinner in town,"
저녁식사
thought she, "and does not eat much for supper,
저녁식사
the bread will last out another day."
끝까지 견디다[가다]
She weighed the piece of bread in her hand
무게를 달다, 따져 보다, 저울질하다
again and again, and thought:
몇 번이고, 되풀이해서
"I won't make any more today. We have only

20

enough flour left to bake one batch; We can manage to make this last out till Friday."

So Matryona put away the bread, and sat down at the table to patch her husband's shirt. While she worked she thought how her husband was buying skins for a winter coat.

"If only the dealer does not cheat him. My good man is much too simple; he cheats no-body, but any child can take him in.

"Eight roubles is a lot of money--he should get a good coat at that price. Not tanned skins, but still a proper winter coat. How difficult it was last winter to get on without a warm coat.

"I could neither get down to the river, nor go out anywhere. When he went out he put on all we had, and there was nothing left for me.

"He did not start very early today, but still it's time he was back. I only hope he has not gone on the spree!"

Hardly had Matryona thought this, when steps were heard on the threshold, and some

one entered. Matryona stuck her needle into her
안으로 들어오다, 입장하다 　　　아무렇게나 급히) 집어넣다(stick)

work and went out into the passage.
통로, 복도(=corridor)

There she saw two men: Simon, and with
보다　2, 둘

him a man without a hat, and wearing felt boots.
모자　　　입다, 신다

Matryona noticed at once that her husband
즉시, 당장

smelt of spirits.
냄새[향]가 나다(smell의 과거·과거분사)

"There now, he has been drinking," thought
마시다

she. And when she saw that he was coatless,
코트를 입지 않은

had only her jacket on, brought no parcel, stood
소포, (선물 등의) 꾸러미

there silent, and seemed ashamed, her heart
조용한, 침묵하는　　　부끄러운, 창피한

was ready to break with disappointment.
실망, 낙심

"He has drunk the money," thought she,

"and has been on the spree with some good-for-
흥청망청 하기, 흥청거리기　　아무 짝에도 쓸모없는

nothing fellow whom he has brought home with

him."

Matryona let them pass into the hut, fol-
(…하게) 놓아두다, (…을 하도록) 허락하다　　(뒤를) 따라가다

lowed them in, and saw that the stranger was a
보다　　　　　낯선[모르는] 사람

young, slight man, wearing her husband's coat.
젊은　야윈, 가냘픈　　입다

There was no shirt to be seen under it, and he
~아래

had no hat.

Having entered, he stood, neither moving,
들어가다, 입장하다　　　~도 아니고 ~도 아니다

22

nor raising his eyes, and Matryona thought: "He
들어올리다
must be a bad man--he's afraid."
나쁜   두려워하다

Matryona frowned, and stood beside the
얼굴을 찡그리다, 눈살을 찌푸리다   ~옆에
oven looking to see what they would do.
오븐, 화덕

Simon took off his cap and sat down on the
벗다   모자   앉다
bench as if things were all right.
마치 ~인 것처럼   괜찮은, 받아들일 만한(=OK)

"Come, Matryona; if supper is ready, let us
저녁 (식사) (하루 끼니 중 마지막에 먹는 것)
have some."

Matryona muttered something to herself
중얼거리다
and did not move, but stayed where she was, by
움직이다   머물다
the oven. She looked first at the one and then at
먼저, 우선, 첫 번째로
the other of them, and only shook her head.
흔들다

Simon saw that his wife was annoyed, but
짜증이 난, 약이 오른(=irritated)
tried to pass it off. Pretending not to notice any-
···인 척하다[것처럼 굴다]   알아차리다, 눈치 채다
thing, he took the stranger by the arm.
팔

"Sit down, friend," said he, "and let us have
앉다   친구   ~하자
some supper."

The stranger sat down on the bench.
벤치, 긴 의자

"Haven't you cooked anything for us?" said
요리하다
Simon.

Matryona's anger boiled over.
하, 분노   끓어 넘치다, 폭발하다(=explode)

23

"I've cooked, but not for you. It seems to me you have drunk your wits away. You went to buy a sheep-skin coat, but come home without so much as the coat you had on, and bring a naked vagabond home with you. I have no supper for drunkards like you."

술을 마시다 / 정신이 나간, 제정신이 아닌 / ~없이 / …조차도, …까지도(even) / 가져오다, 데려오다 / 방랑자, 떠돌이 / 술고래 (=alcoholic)

"That's enough, Matryona. Don't wag your tongue without reason. You had better ask what sort of man--"

이제 됐다! 그쯤 해둬! / 흔들다, 놀리다 / 혀 / 이유, 까닭, 근거 / 더 나은 / 묻다 / 종류, 부류

"And you tell me what you've done with the money?"

말하다, 알리다

Simon found the pocket of the jacket, drew out the three-rouble note, and unfolded it.

주머니 / 꺼내다 / 3루블 / 지폐 / (접혀 있는 것을) 펴다[펼치다]

"Here is the money. Trifonof did not pay, but promises to pay soon."

지불하다 / 약속하다 / 곧

Matryona got still more angry; he had bought no sheep-skins, but had put his only coat on some naked fellow and had even brought him to their house.

화나다, 분노하다 / 사다(buy) / 유일한

She snatched up the note from the table, took it to put away in safety, and said:

와락 붙잡다, 잡아채다 / 지폐 / 식탁 / 안전한 곳

"I have no supper for you. We can't feed all the naked drunkards in the world."

"There now, Matryona, hold your tongue a bit. First hear what a man has to say-"

"Much wisdom I shall hear from a drunken fool. I was right in not wanting to marry you- a drunkard. The linen my mother gave me you drank; and now you've been to buy a coat-and have drunk it, too!"

Simon tried to explain to his wife that he had only spent twenty kopeks; tried to tell how he had found the man--but Matryona would not let him get a word in. She talked nineteen to the dozen, and dragged in things that had happened ten years before.

Matryona talked and talked, and at last she flew at Simon and seized him by the sleeve.

"Give me my jacket. It is the only one I have, and you must needs take it from me and wear it yourself. Give it here, you mangy dog, and may the devil take you."

Simon began to pull off the jacket, and
시작하다   벗다

turned a sleeve of it inside out; Matryona seized
소매

the jacket and it burst its seams, She snatched it
터지다   솔기   잡아 채다

up, threw it over her head and went to the door.
던지다   ~위로   문

She meant to go out, but stopped undecided-
의미하다, …의 뜻이다(mean)   결정하지 못한, 결심이 서지 않은

-she wanted to work off her anger, but she also
원하다, 바라다   (강한 감정을 육체적인 노력을 통하여) 풀다   또한

wanted to learn what sort of a man the stranger
알다, 배우다   종류, 부류

was.

4

Matryona stopped and said:

"If he were a good man he would not be naked. Why, he hasn't even a shirt on him. If he were all right, you would say where you came across the fellow."

"That's just what I am trying to tell you," said Simon. "As I came to the shrine I saw him sitting all naked and frozen. It isn't quite the weather to sit about naked! God sent me to him, or he would have perished.

"What was I to do? How do we know what may have happened to him? So I took him, clothed him, and brought him along.

"Don't be so angry, Matryona. It is a sin. (화내다 / 죄, 죄악) Remember, we all must die one day." (기억하라 / 모두 / 죽다 / 언젠가)

Angry words rose to Matryona's lips, but she (성난 말, 격한 말 / 일어나다, 오르다 / 입술) looked at the stranger and was silent. He sat on (~를 쳐다보다 / 낯선 사람 / 침묵하다) the edge of the bench, motionless, his hands (~가, 끝 / 긴 의자 / 움직이지 않는) folded on his knees, his head drooping on his (접다, 포개다 / 무릎 / 아래로 처지다[늘어지다]) breast, his eyes closed, and his brows knit as if (가슴 / 눈썹) in pain. Matryona was silent: and Simon said: (아픈, 괴로운, 고통스러운)

"Matryona, have you no love of God?"

Matryona heard these words, and as she looked at the stranger, suddenly her heart soft- (갑자기, 별안간 / 마음) ened towards him. She came back from the (~을 향해) door, and going to the oven she got out the sup- (오븐, 화덕 / 저녁을 내오다) per. Setting a cup on the table, she poured out (차리다 / 쏟다, 붓다) some kvas. Then she brought out the last piece (크바스(보리·엿기름·호밀로 만드는 맥주 비슷한 러시아의 음료)) of bread, and set out a knife and spoons.

"Eat, if you want to," said she.

Simon drew the stranger to the table. (끌다, 끌어당기다)

"Take your place, young man," said he. (자리를 잡아라)

Simon cut the bread, crumbled it into the (자르다 / 바스러뜨리다) broth, and they began to eat. ((걸쭉한) 수프, 죽)

Matryona sat at the corner of the table resting her head on her hand and looking at the stranger.

And Matryona was touched with pity for the stranger, and began to feel fond of him. And at once the stranger's face lit up; his brows were no longer bent, he raised his eyes and smiled at Matryona.

When they had finished supper, the woman cleared away the things and began questioning the stranger.

"Where are you from?" said she.

"I am not from these parts."

"But how did you come to be on the road?"

"I may not tell."

"Did some one rob you?"

"God punished me."

"And you were lying there naked?"

"Yes, naked and freezing. Simon saw me and had pity on me. He took off his coat, put it on me and brought me here. And you have fed me,

29

given me drink, and shown pity on me. God will

reward you!"

보상하다, 보답하다, 사례하다

Matryona rose, took from the window Si-

일어나다

mon's old shirt she had been patching, and gave

오래된, 낡은   (헝겊 등으로) 덧대다(=mend)

it to the stranger. She also brought out a pair of

trousers for him.

바지

"There," said she, "I see you have no shirt.

Put this on, and lie down where you please, in

입다   눕다

the loft or on the oven."

고미다락(→attic, garret)

The stranger took off the coat, put on the

벗다   입다

shirt, and lay down in the loft. Matryona put out

눕다

the candle, took the coat, and climbed to where

초, 양초   오르다, 올라가다

her husband lay.

Matryona drew the skirts of the coat over

끌어당기다   코트 자락

her and lay down, but could not sleep; she could

잠들다

not get the stranger out of her mind.

When she remembered that he had eaten

기억하다, 생각나다

their last piece of bread and that there was none

마지막   조각   아무 것도 없는

for tomorrow, and thought of the shirt and trou-

셔츠   바지

sers she had given away, she felt grieved; but

줘버리다   대단히 슬픈(=pain)

when she remembered how he had smiled, her

heart was glad.

Long did Matryona lie awake, and she noticed that Simon also was awake--he drew the
coat towards him.

"Simon!"

"Well?"

"You have had the last of the bread, and I
have not put any to rise. I don't know what we
shall do tomorrow. Perhaps I can borrow some
of neighbor Martha."

"If we're alive we shall find something to
eat."

The woman lay still awhile, and then said,
"He seems a good man, but why does he not tell
us who he is?"

"I suppose he has his reasons."

"Simon!"

"Well?"

"We give; but why does nobody give us anything?"

Simon did not know what to say; so he only
알다   오직, 그저
said, "Let us stop talking," and turned over and
~하자   멈추다, 그만 두다   돌아 눕다
went to sleep.

5

In the morning Simon awoke. The children were still asleep; his wife had gone to the neighbor's to borrow some bread.

The stranger alone was sitting on the bench, dressed in the old shirt and trousers, and looking upwards. His face was brighter than it had been the day before.

Simon said to him, "Well, friend; the belly wants bread, and the naked body clothes. One has to work for a living What work do you know?"

"I do not know any."

This surprised Simon, but he said, "Men who

want to learn can learn anything."

"Men work, and I will work also."

"What is your name?"

"Michael."

"Well, Michael, if you don't wish to talk about yourself, that is your own affair; but you'll have to earn a living for yourself. If you will work as I tell you, I will give you food and shelter."

"May God reward you! I will learn. Show me what to do."

Simon took yarn, put it round his thumb and began to twist it.

"It is easy enough--see!"

Michael watched him, put some yarn round his own thumb in the same way, caught the knack, and twisted the yarn also.

Then Simon showed him how to wax the thread. This also Michael mastered. Next Simon showed him how to twist the bristle in, and how to sew, and this, too, Michael learned at once.

Whatever Simon showed him he understood
어떤 …일지라도, 어떤 …이든   이해하다
at once, and after three days he worked as if he
~뒤에   일하다   마치 ~인 것처럼
had sewn boots all his life.
바느질하다, 깁다(sew)
He worked without stopping, and ate little.
eat의 과거
When work was over he sat silently, looking
끝나다, 마치다   아무 말없이, 조용히(=quietly)
upwards. He hardly went into the street, spoke
거의...아니다[없다]   거리
only when necessary, and neither joked nor
필요한(=essential), 불가피한(=inevitable)   농담하다
laughed.
웃다
They never saw him smile, except that first
~을 제외하고는(= apart from)
evening when Matryona gave them supper.

6

Day by day and week by week the year
went round. Michael lived and worked
with Simon. His fame spread till people said
that no one sewed boots so neatly and strongly
as Simon's workman, Michael; and from all the
district round people came to Simon for their
boots, and he began to be well off.

One winter day, as Simon and Michael sat
working, a carriage on sledge-runners, with
three horses and with bells, drove up to the hut.
They looked out of the window; the carriage
stopped at their door, a fine servant jumped
down from the box and opened the door.

A gentleman in a fur coat got out and walked up to Simon's hut. Up jumped Matryona and opened the door wide.

The gentleman stooped to enter the hut, and when he drew himself up again his head nearly reached the ceiling, and he seemed quite to fill his end of the room.

Simon rose, bowed, and looked at the gentleman with astonishment. He had never seen any one like him. Simon himself was lean, Michael was thin, and Matryona was dry as a bone, but this man was like some one from another world: red-faced, burly, with a neck like a bull's, and looking altogether as if he were cast in iron.

The gentleman puffed, threw off his fur coat, sat down on the bench, and said, "Which of you is the master bootmaker?"

"I am, your Excellency," said Simon, coming forward.

Then the gentleman shouted to his lad, "Hey, Fedka, bring the leather!"

The servant ran in, bringing a parcel. The
gentleman took the parcel and put it on the
table.

"Untie it," said he.

The lad untied it.

The gentleman pointed to the leather.

"Look here, shoemaker," said he, "do you see
this leather?"

"Yes, your honor."

"But do you know what sort of leather it is?"

Simon felt the leather and said, "It is good
leather."

"Good, indeed! Why, you fool, you never saw
such leather before in your life. It's German, and
cost twenty roubles."

Simon was frightened, and said, "Where
should I ever see leather like that?"

"Just so! Now, can you make it into boots for
me?"

"Yes, your Excellency, I can."

Then the gentleman shouted at him:

"You can, can you? Well, remember whom
you are to make them for, and what the leather
is. You must make me boots that will wear for a
year, neither losing shape nor coming unsown.
"If you can do it, take the leather and cut it
up; but if you can't, say so. I warn you now if
your boots become unsewn or lose shape within
a year, I will have you put in prison. If they don't
burst or lose shape for a year I will pay you ten
roubles for your work."

Simon was frightened, and did not know
what to say. He glanced at Michael and nudging
him with his elbow, whispered: "Shall I take the
work?"

Michael nodded his head as if to say, "Yes,
take it."

Simon did as Michael advised, and under-
took to make boots that would not lose shape
or split for a whole year. Calling his servant, the
gentleman told him to pull the boot off his left
leg, which he stretched out.

"Take my measure!" said he.

(치수 등을 표준 단위로) 측정하다[재다]

Simon stitched a paper measure seventeen

바느질하다, 꿰매다, 깁다(=sew)

inches long, smoothed it out, knelt down, wiped

반듯하게 펴다   무릎을 꿇다(kneel)

his hand well on his apron so as not to soil the

앞치마   더럽히다

gentleman's sock, and began to measure.

양말   재다, 측정하다

He measured the sole, and round the instep,

재다   발바닥   (신발의) 발등 (부분)

and began to measure the calf of the leg, but the

종아리   다리

paper was too short. The calf of the leg was as

종이   짧은

thick as a beam.

두꺼운   기둥

"Mind you don't make it too tight in the leg."

꽉 조이는, 딱 붙는

Simon stitched on another strip of paper.

바느질하다   또 다른   가느다란 조각

The gentleman twitched his toes about in his

씰룩거리다, 경련하다   발가락

sock, looking round at those in the hut, and as

양말   주위를 둘러보다

he did so he noticed Michael.

알아차리다, 주목하다

"Whom have you there?" asked he.

"That is my workman. He will sew the

일꾼   꿰매다, 깁다

boots."

"Mind," said the gentleman to Michael, "re-

member to make them so that they will last me

만들다   오래가다, 질기다

a year."

Simon also looked at Michael, and saw that

또한, 역시   ~을 쳐다보다

Michael was not looking at the gentleman, but was gazing into the corner behind the gentle-
응시하다   구석, 모서리   ~뒤에
man, as if he saw some one there. Michael
마치 ~인 것처럼
looked and looked, and suddenly he smiled, and
보고 또 보다   갑자기, 돌연
his face became brighter.
더 밝아지다, 더 환해지다

"What are you grinning at, you fool?" thun-
(소리 없이) 활짝[크게] 웃다   (큰 소리로) 고함치다
dered the gentleman. "You had better look to it
that the boots are ready in time."
제 때에, 때 맞춰서

"They shall be ready in good time," said Mi-
준비되다
chael.

"Mind it is so," said the gentleman, and he
put on his boots and his fur coat, wrapped the
신다   모피 코트   감싸다
latter round him, and went to the door. But he
후자
forgot to stoop, and struck his head against the
잊다, 잊어버리다   (몸을) 구부리다   세게 치다, 때리다
lintel.
상인방(문·창문을 가로지르는 가로대)
He swore and rubbed his head. Then he took
욕하다   비비다, 문지르다
his seat in the carriage and drove away.
~몰고 떠나다

When he had gone, Simon said: "There's a
figure of a man for you! You could not kill him
몸집, 체격, 모습   죽이다
with a mallet. He almost knocked out the lintel,
나무망치   거의
but little harm it did him."
해롭 끼치다, 다치게 하다

41

And Matryona said: "Living as he does, how should he not grow strong? Death itself can't
강한, 힘센   죽음
touch such a rock as that."
건드리다, 손대다   바위

7

Then Simon said to Michael:

"Well, we have taken the work, but we must see we don't get into trouble over it. The leather is dear, and the gentleman hot-tempered. We must make no mistakes.

"Come, your eye is truer and your hands have become nimbler than mine, so you take this measure and cut out the boots. I will finish off the sewing of the vamps."

Michael did as he was told. He took the leather, spread it out on the table, folded it in two, took a knife and began to cut out.

Matryona came and watched him cutting,
(관심을 갖고) 지켜보다
and was surprised to see how he was doing
깜짝 놀라다
it. Matryona was accustomed to seeing boots
(…에) 익숙해지다, 길들다
made, and she looked and saw that Michael was

not cutting the leather for boots, but was cutting

it round.
둥글게, 동그랗게
　　She wished to say something, but she
바라다, 원하다
thought to herself: "Perhaps I do not under-
아마, 어쩌면   알다, 이해하다
stand how gentleman's boots should be made.

I suppose Michael knows more about it--and I
추정하다, 짐작하다
won't interfere."
간섭하다, 개입하다, 참견하다
　　When Michael had cut up the leather, he

took a thread and began to sew not with two
실   바느질하다, 깁다
ends, as boots are sewn, but with a single end,

as for soft slippers. Again Matryona wondered,
부드러운 슬리퍼   의아해 하다, 궁금해 하다
but again she did not interfere. Michael sewed
간섭하다, 참견하다
on steadily till noon.
꾸준히, 야무지게   정오
　　Then Simon rose for dinner, looked around,
일어나다   주위를 둘러보다
and saw that Michael had made slippers out of

the gentleman's leather.

"Ah," groaned Simon, and he thought,
신음[끙 하는] 소리를 내다
"How is it that Michael, who has been with me
a whole year and never made a mistake before,
실수, 잘못
should do such a dreadful thing? The gentleman
끔찍한, 지독한
ordered high boots, welted, with whole fronts,
주문하다   (목이 긴) 장화   (구두창의) 대다리를 댄
and Michael has made soft slippers with single
soles, and has wasted the leather. What am I to
발바닥   낭비하다
say to the gentleman? I can never replace leath-
대신[대체]하다
er such as this."

And he said to Michael, "What are you doing, friend? You have ruined me! You know the
망치다[엉망으로 만들다](=wreck)
gentleman ordered high boots, but see what you
주문하다
have made!"

Hardly had he begun to rebuke Michael,
힐책[질책]하다, 꾸짖다
when "rat-tat" went the iron ring that hung at
쇠   종   매달린
the door. Some one was knocking. They looked
문을 두드리다, 노크하다
out of the window; a man had come on horse-
창문
back, and was fastening his horse. They opened
매다, 채우다
the door, and the servant who had been with the
하인
gentleman came in.

"Good day," said he.

"Good day," replied Simon. "What can we do
for you?"

"My mistress has sent me about the boots."
"What about the boots?"

"Why, my master no longer needs them. He
is dead."

"Is it possible?"

"He did not live to get home after leaving
you, but died in the carriage. When we reached
home and the servants came to help him alight,
he rolled over like a sack. He was dead already,
and so stiff that he could hardly be got out of the
carriage.

"My mistress sent me here, saying:

'Tell the bootmaker that the gentleman who
ordered boots of him and left the leather for
them no longer needs the boots, but that he
must quickly make soft slippers for the corpse.
Wait till they are ready, and bring them back
with you.'

That is why I have come."

Michael gathered up the remnants of the
leather; rolled them up, took the soft slippers he
had made, slapped them together, wiped them
down with his apron, and handed them and the
roll of leather to the servant, who took them and
said:

"Good-bye, masters, and good day to you!"

47

8

Another year passed, and another, and Michael was now living his sixth year with
또 하나(의); 더, 또   지나가다   6년
Simon. He lived as before.

He went nowhere, only spoke when
            아무 데도 (···않다)
necessary, and had only smiled twice in all those
필요한(=essential), 필연적인, 불가피한(=inevitable)   2번
years--once when Matryona gave him food, and
                              주다   음식
a second time when the gentleman was in their
제2의, 둘째 (번)의
hut.

Simon was more than pleased with his work-
            ···보다 많이, ···이상(의)
man. He never now asked him where he came
                    묻다
from, and only feared lest Michael should go
            (···을) 두려워[무서워]하다
away.

They were all at home one day. Matryona
        모두   어느 날

was putting iron pots in the oven; the children
가마솥, (쇠로 된) 솥[냄비]

were running along the benches and looking out
…을 따라   벤치, 긴의자

of the window; Simon was sewing at one win-
창문   바느질하다, 꿰매다

dow, and Michael was fastening on a heel at the
(움직이지 않게) 고정시키다

other. One of the boys ran along the bench to

Michael, leant on his shoulder, and looked out
~에 기대다(LEAN의 과거·과거분사)

of the window.

"Look, Uncle Michael! There is a lady with
숙녀

little girls! She seems to be coming here. And
소녀   (…인·하는 것처럼) 보이다, …인[하는] 것 같다(=appear)

one of the girls is lame."
다리를 저는, 절뚝거리는

When the boy said that, Michael dropped his
떨어지다, 떨어뜨리다

work, turned to the window, and looked out into

the street.
거리

Simon was surprised. Michael never used
깜짝 놀라다   ~하곤 하다

to look out into the street, but now he pressed
바짝 대다, 밀착시키다

against the window, staring at something.
~을 응시하다, ~을 뻔히 쳐다보다

Simon also looked out, and saw that a well-
(옷을) 잘 차려 입은

dressed woman was really coming to his hut,
부인   정말로, 실제로

leading by the hand two little girls in fur coats
이끌다   모피, 털

and woolen shawls.
양모의   숄

49

The girls could hardly be told one from the
other, except that one of them was crippled in
her left leg and walked with a limp.
The woman stepped into the porch and
entered the passage. Feeling about for the en-
trance she found the latch, which she lifted, and
opened the door. She let the two girls go in first,
and followed them into the hut.

"Good day, good folk!"

"Pray come in," said Simon. "What can we
do for you?"

The woman sat down by the table. The two
little girls pressed close to her knees, afraid of
the people in the hut.

"I want leather shoes made for these two
little girls for spring."

"We can do that. We never have made such
small shoes, but we can make them; either
welted or turnover shoes, linen lined. My man,
Michael, is a master at the work."

Simon glanced at Michael and saw that he had left his work and was sitting with his eyes fixed on the little girls.

Simon was surprised. It was true the girls were pretty, with black eyes, plump, and rosy-cheeked, and they wore nice kerchiefs and fur coats, but still Simon could not understand why Michael should look at them like that--just as if he had known them before.

He was puzzled, but went on talking with the woman, and arranging the price.

Having fixed it, he prepared the measure. The woman lifted the lame girl on to her lap and said:

"Take two measures from this little girl. Make one shoe for the lame foot and three for the sound one. They both have the same size feet. They are twins."

Simon took the measure and, speaking of the lame girl, said: "How did it happen to her? She is such a pretty girl. Was she born so?"

"No, her mother crushed her leg."

Then Matryona joined in. She wondered who this woman was, and whose the children were, so she said: "Are not you their mother then?"

"No, my good woman; I am neither their mother nor any relation to them. They were quite strangers to me, but I adopted them."

"They are not your children and yet you are so fond of them?"

"How can I help being fond of them? I fed them both at my own breasts. I had a child of my own, but God took him. I was not so fond of him as I now am of them."

"Then whose children are they?"

9

The woman, having begun talking, told them the whole story.

"It is about six years since their parents died, both in one week: their father was buried on the Tuesday, and their mother died on the Friday. These orphans were born three days after their father's death, and their mother did not live another day.

"My husband and I were then living as peasants in the village. We were neighbors of theirs, our yard being next to theirs. Their father was a lonely man; a wood-cutter in the forest. When felling trees one day, they let one fall on

him. It fell across his body and crushed his bow-
fall   으깨다, 부수다   창자, 장
els out.

"They hardly got him home before his soul
거의 ~할 수 없다   영혼
went to God; and that same week his wife gave
같은   아내   ~을 낳다
birth to twins--these little girls.
쌍둥이

"She was poor and alone; she had no one,
혼자, 다른 사람 없이
young or old, with her. Alone she gave them

birth, and alone she met her death.
만나다, 마주하다(meet)

"The next morning I went to see her, but
다음날 아침
when I entered the hut, she, poor thing, was al-
들어가다   가엾은, 불쌍한
ready stark and cold. In dying she had rolled on
차갑게 굳은   ~위로 구르다
to this child and crushed her leg.

"The village folk came to the hut, washed
마을 사람들   씻다, 씻기다
the body, laid her out, made a coffin, and buried
시신   관   묻다
her. They were good folk. The babies were left
(일반적인) 사람들   홀로 남겨지다
alone. What was to be done with them?

"I was the only woman there who had a baby
유일한, 단 하나의
at the time. I was nursing my first-born--eight
그 당시에   젖을 먹이다, 보살피다
weeks old. So I took them for a time.
한동안, 잠시

"The peasants came together, and thought
농부   함께   곰곰이 생각하다
and thought what to do with them; and at last
마침내, 결국

54

they said to me: 'For the present, Mary, you had better keep the girls, and later on we will arrange what to do for them.'

"So I nursed the sound one at my breast, but at first I did not feed this crippled one. I did not suppose she would live. But then I thought to myself, why should the poor innocent suffer? I pitied her, and began to feed her. And so I fed my own boy and these two--the three of them-- at my own breast.

"I was young and strong, and had good food, and God gave me so much milk that at times it even overflowed. I used sometimes to feed two at a time, while the third was waiting.

"When one had enough I nursed the third. And God so ordered it that these grew up, while my own was buried before he was two years old. And I had no more children, though we prospered.

"Now my husband is working for the corn merchant at the mill. The pay is good, and we

현재로서는, 당장은, 당분간은 · 나중에, 뒤에 · 배열하다, 마련하다, 주선하다 · 젖을 먹이다, 보살피다 · 처음에 · 먹이다 · 불구의, 무능력한 · 짐작하다, 추정하다 · 아무 잘못 없는 것 시달리다; 고통받다 · 동정하다, 연민을 느끼다 · 젊은 · 강한 · 질 좋은 음식을 먹다 · 넘치다, 넘쳐흐르다 · 때때로, 간혹 · 한 번에 · 세 번째, 셋째 · 기다리다 · 충분히 · 젖을 먹이다 · 명령하다, 지시하다 · 자라다, 성장하다 · 묻다 · ~전에 · 번영[번창/번성]하다 · 남편 · ~에서 근무하다[일하다] · 곡물 · 상인, 부엌상 · 방앗간, 제분소 · 보수, 사례

are well off. But I have no children of my own, and how lonely I should be without these little girls! How can I help loving them! They are the joy of my life!"

She pressed the lame little girl to her with one hand, while with the other she wiped the tears from her cheeks.

And Matryona sighed, and said: "The proverb is true that says, 'One may live without father or mother, but one cannot live without God.'"

So they talked together, when suddenly the whole hut was lighted up as though by summer lightning from the corner where Michael sat. They all looked towards him and saw him sitting, his hands folded on his knees, gazing upwards and smiling.

10

The woman went away with the girls. Michael rose from the bench, put down his work, and took off his apron. Then, bowing low to Simon and his wife, he said:

"Farewell, masters. God has forgiven me. I ask your forgiveness, too, for anything done amiss."

And they saw that a light shone from Michael. And Simon rose, bowed down to Michael, and said:

"I see, Michael, that you are no common man, and I can neither keep you nor question you. Only tell me this: how is it that when

I found you and brought you home, you were
발견하다 데려오다
gloomy, and when my wife gave you food you
우울한, 침울한
smiled at her and became brighter?
~를 보고 미소 짓다   더 환해지다
    "Then when the gentleman came to order
                                        주문하다
the boots, you smiled again and became brighter still? And now, when this woman brought
the little girls, you smiled a third time, and have
                                세 번째로
become as bright as day? Tell me, Michael, why
does your face shine so, and why did you smile
          얼굴   빛나다, 반짝이다
those three times?"

    And Michael answered:
              대답하다
    "Light shines from me because I have been
punished, but now God has pardoned me. And
처벌하다, 벌주다   용서하다, 사면하다
I smiled three times, because God sent me to
                                보내다
learn three truths, and I have learnt them. One
배우다   진실, 진리
I learnt when your wife pitied me, and that is
                    동정하다, 연민을 느끼다
why I smiled the first time. The second I learnt
when the rich man ordered the boots, and then
              부유한
I smiled again. And now, when I saw those
little girls, I learn the third and last truth, and I
                                마지막
smiled the third time."

And Simon said, "Tell me, Michael, what did
God punish you for? and what were the three
벌주다   무엇 때문에?
truths? that I, too, may know them."

And Michael answered:

"God punished me for disobeying Him. I
불복종, 저항, 반항
was an angel in heaven and disobeyed God. God
천사   천국, 하늘나라   복종하지 않다, 저항하다
sent me to fetch a woman's soul. I flew to earth,
데리고 오다   영혼   날아가다   땅, 지구
and saw a sick woman lying alone, who had just
아픈, 병든   홀로, 외로이   막 아이를 낳다
given birth to twin girls. They moved feebly at
쌍둥이   움직이다   약하게, 힘없이
their mother's side, but she could not lift them
들어올리다
to her breast.
가슴

"When she saw me, she understood that God
이해하다, 알다
had sent me for her soul, and she wept and said:
보내다   영혼   울다
'Angel of God! My husband has just been
천사   남편
buried, killed by a falling tree. I have neither
묻다   죽임을 당하다 쓰러진, 넘어진   ~도 ~도 없는
sister, nor aunt, nor mother: no one to care for
여자형제   숙모, 고모, 이모 어머니   돌보다, 보살피다
my orphans. Do not take my soul! Let me nurse
고아   ~하게 하다
my babes, feed them, and set them on their feet
먹이다
before I die. Children cannot live without father
~없이 살다
or mother.'

"And I hearkened to her. I placed one child
귀 기울여 듣다   (조심스럽게) 놓다[두다]

at her breast and gave the other into her arms, and returned to the Lord in heaven.

"I flew to the Lord, and said:

'I could not take the soul of the mother. Her husband was killed by a tree; the woman has twins, and prays that her soul may not be taken. She says:

"Let me nurse and feed my children, and set them on their feet. Children cannot live without father or mother." I have not taken her soul.'

"And God said:

'Go-take the mother's soul, and learn three truths: Learn What dwells in man, What is not given to man, and What men live by. When thou has learnt these things, thou shalt return to heaven.'

"So I flew again to earth and took the mother's soul. The babes dropped from her breasts. Her body rolled over on the bed and crushed one babe, twisting its leg. I rose above the village, wishing to take her soul to God; but a wind seized me, and my wings drooped and dropped

꽉 붙잡다 　　　　　　　　날개 　　아래로 처지다[늘어지다]　 떨어져 나가다

off. Her soul rose alone to God, while I fell to

혼자 힘으로

earth by the roadside."

길가, 도로변

11

And Simon and Matryona understood
이해하다
who it was that had lived with them, and
~와 함께 살다
whom they had clothed and fed. And they wept
옷을 입히다　　먹을 것을 주다　　울다
with awe and with joy. And the angel said:
경외감, 외경심　　기쁨, 환희　　천사

"I was alone in the field, naked. I had never
홀로, 외로이　　들판　　벌거벗은
known human needs, cold and hunger, till I be-
인간　　필요, 욕구　　추위　　굶주림　　~까지
came a man. I was famished, frozen, and did not
굶주리게 하다(starve)　　꽁꽁 얼어붙다
know what to do.

"I saw, near the field I was in, a shrine built
근처, 가까운　　성소, 교회, 성당
for God, and I went to it hoping to find shelter.
바라다　　피난처, 대피소
But the shrine was locked, and I could not enter.
잠그다　　들어가다
So I sat down behind the shrine to shelter my-
~뒤에
self at least from the wind. Evening drew on.
적어도, 최소한　　저녁

"I was hungry, frozen, and in pain. Suddenly I heard a man coming along the road. He carried a pair of boots, and was talking to himself. For the first time since I became a man I saw the mortal face of a man, and his face seemed terrible to me and I turned from it.

"And I heard the man talking to himself of how to cover his body from the cold in winter, and how to feed wife and children.

"And I thought: 'I am perishing of cold and hunger, and here is a man thinking only of how to clothe himself and his wife, and how to get bread for themselves. He cannot help me.'

"When the man saw me he frowned and became still more terrible, and passed me by on the other side. I despaired; but suddenly I heard him coming back.

"I looked up, and did not recognize the same man; before, I had seen death in his face; but now he was alive, and I recognized in him the presence of God.

아픈, 고통스러운 / 듣다 / ~을 따라 / 길, 도로 / 나르다, 운반하다 / 장화 / 처음으로, 첫 번째로 / ~이후에 / ~가 되다 / 영원히 살 수는 없는, 언젠가는 반드시 죽는 / 끔찍한, 소름끼치는 / 돌리다 / 듣다 / 혼잣말하다 / 덮다, 가리다 / 몸, 육체 / 추위 / 음식을 먹이다 / (끔찍하게) 죽다, 비명횡사하다 / 오직, 그저 / 얻다 / 얼굴을 찌푸리다, 눈살을 찡그리다 / 더욱 / 끔찍한 / 지나치다 / 절망하다, 체념하다 / 갑자기 / 돌아오다 / 알아보다, 알다 / 죽음 / 살아 있는 / 존재, 현존

"He came up to me, clothed me, took me
with him, and brought me to his home.

"I entered the house; a woman came to
meet us and began to speak. The woman was
still more terrible than the man had been; the
spirit of death came from her mouth; I could
not breathe for the stench of death that spread
around her. She wished to drive me out into the
cold, and I knew that if she did so she would die.

"Suddenly her husband spoke to her of God,
and the woman changed at once. And when she
brought me food and looked at me, I glanced at
her and saw that death no longer dwelt in her;
she had become alive, and in her, too, I saw
God.

"Then I remembered the first lesson God
had set me: 'Learn what dwells in man.'

"And I understood that in man dwells Love!
I was glad that God had already begun to show
me what He had promised, and I smiled for the
first time.

"But I had not yet learnt all. I did not yet know What is not given to man, and What men live by.

"I lived with you, and a year passed. A man came to order boots that should wear for a year without losing shape or cracking. I looked at him, and suddenly, behind his shoulder, I saw my comrade--the angel of death.

"None but me saw that angel; but I knew him, and knew that before the sun set he would take that rich man's soul. And I thought to myself, 'The man is making preparations for a year, and does not know that he will die before evening.' "And I remembered God's second saying, 'Learn what is not given to man.'

"What dwells in man I already knew. Now I learnt what is not given him. It is not given to man to know his own needs. And I smiled for the second time. I was glad to have seen my comrade angel--glad also that God had revealed to me the second saying.

"But I still did not know all. I did not know What men live by. And I lived on, waiting till 기다리다 God should reveal to me the last lesson. 드러내 보이다   마지막 교훈
"In the sixth year came the girl-twins with 쌍둥이 소녀 the woman; and I recognized the girls, and 인지하다, 알다 heard how they had been kept alive. Hav- 듣다   살아 있는 ing heard the story, I thought, 'Their mother 이야기 besought me for the children's sake, and I be- 간청하다, 애원하다(=implore, beg)   ~ 때문에[~를 위해서] lieved her when she said that children cannot live without father or mother; but a stranger has 낯선 사람 nursed them, and has brought them up.' 젖을 먹이다   기르다, 양육하다
"And when the woman showed her love for 부인, 여자   보여주다   사랑 the children that were not her own, and wept 울다 over them, I saw in her the living God and un- 살아 있는 신, 현존하는 신 derstood What men live by.

"And I knew that God had revealed to me 드러내 보여주다 the last lesson, and had forgiven my sin. And 마지막 교훈   용서하다   죄, 죄악 then I smiled for the third time."

12

And the angel's body was bared, and he was clothed in light so that eye could not look on him; and his voice grew louder, as though it came not from him but from heaven above. And the angel said:

"I have learnt that all men live not by care for themselves but by love.

"It was not given to the mother to know what her children needed for their life. Nor was it given to the rich man to know what he himself needed. Nor is it given to any man to know whether, when evening comes, he will need boots for his body or slippers for his corpse.

"I remained alive when I was a man, not by
살아 남다
care of myself, but because love was present in
돌봄, 보살핌   ~때문에
a passer-by, and because he and his wife pitied
행인, 지나가는 사람
and loved me.

"The orphans remained alive not because of
고아   살아 남다
their mother's care, but because there was love
in the heart of a woman, a stranger to them,
마음   낯선 사람, 모르는 이
who pitied and loved them. And all men live not
동정하는, 불쌍히 여기는
by the thought they spend on their own welfare,
쓰다, 소비하다   (개인의) 안녕[행복]
but because love exists in man.
존재[실재/현존]하다
"I knew before that God gave life to men
생명
and desires that they should live; now I under-
바라다, 욕구하다
stood more than that. I understood that God
~이상의
does not wish men to live apart, and therefore
바라다, 원하다   따로, 헤어져   그러므로
he does not reveal to them what each one needs
드러내다   각자, 각각의
for himself; but he wishes them to live united,
단결한, 합심한
and therefore reveals to each of them what is
necessary for all.
필연적인, 불가피한
"I have now understood that though it seems
to men that they live by care for themselves, in
돌봄, 보살핌
truth it is love alone by which they live.
진실, 참

"He who has love, is in God, and God is in him, for God is love."

And the angel sang praise to God, so that the hut trembled at his voice. The roof opened, and a column of fire rose from earth to heaven. Simon and his wife and children fell to the ground. Wings appeared upon the angel's shoulders, and he rose into the heavens.

And when Simon came to himself the hut stood as before, and there was no one in it but his own family.

세 가지 질문

THREE QUESTIONS

It once occurred to a certain king, that if he always knew the right time to begin every-thing; if he knew who were the right people to listen to, and whom to avoid; and, above all, if he always knew what was the most important thing to do, he would never fail in anything he might undertake.

And this thought having occurred to him, he had it proclaimed throughout his kingdom that he would give a great reward to any one who would teach him what was the right time for every action, and who were the most necessary people, and how he might know what was the most important thing to do.

And learned men came to the King, but they all answered his questions differently.

In reply to the first question, some said that to know the right time for every action, one must draw up in advance, a table of days, months and years, and must live strictly according to it. Only thus, said they, could everything be done at its proper time.

Others declared that it was impossible to decide beforehand the right time for every action; but that, not letting oneself be absorbed in idle pastimes, one should always attend to all that was going on, and then do what was most needful. Others, again, said that however attentive the King might be to what was going on, it was impossible for one man to decide correctly the right time for every action, but that he should have a Council of wise men, who would help him to fix the proper time for everything.

But then again others said there were some things which could not wait to be laid before a Council, but about which one had at once to decide whether to undertake them or not. But in order to decide that, one must know beforehand what was going to happen. It is only magicians who know that; and, therefore, in order to know the right time for every action, one must consult magicians.

Equally various were the answers to the second question. Some said, the people the King most needed were his councillors; others, the priests; others, the doctors; while some said the warriors were the most necessary.

To the third question, as to what was the most important occupation: some replied that the most important thing in the world was science. Others said it was skill in warfare; and others, again, that it was religious worship.

All the answers being different, the King agreed with none of them, and gave the reward

74

to none. But still wishing to find the right an-
바라다   찾다
swers to his questions, he decided to consult a
결심하다, 결정하다   상담하다, 의논하다
hermit, widely renowned for his wisdom.
은둔자   널리 알려진   지혜, 슬기

The hermit lived in a wood which he never
숲, 삼림
quitted, and he received none but common folk.
(살던 곳을) 떠나다   받아들이다, 맞이하다, 접대하다   보통의, 일반적인 사람들
So the King put on simple clothes, and before
입다   단순한, 소박한
reaching the hermit's cell dismounted from his
닿다, 도착하다   수도실, 암자   ~에서 내리다
horse, and, leaving his body-guard behind, went
경호원
on alone.
혼자

When the King approached, the hermit was
다가가다, 접근하다
digging the ground in front of his hut. Seeing
파다   땅바닥   ~앞에 있는   오두막
the King, he greeted him and went on digging.
인사하다   ~을 계속하다
The hermit was frail and weak, and each time
노쇠한   약한, 힘이 없는
he stuck his spade into the ground and turned a
찌르다, 박다   가래, 삽   흙을 뒤집다
little earth, he breathed heavily.
거칠게 숨 쉬다, 헐떡거리다

The King went up to him and said: "I have
…으로 (가까이) 가다
come to you, wise hermit, to ask you to answer
현명한   은둔자   대답하다
three questions: How can I learn to do the right
알다, 배우다
thing at the right time? Who are the people I
most need, and to whom should I, therefore, pay
필요한
more attention than to the rest? And, what af-
관심, 주의   니미지, 다른 사람들

fairs are the most important, and need my first
attention?"

The hermit listened to the King, but answered nothing. He just spat on his hand and
recommenced digging.

"You are tired," said the King, "let me take
the spade and work awhile for you."

"Thanks!" said the hermit, and, giving the
spade to the King, he sat down on the ground.

When he had dug two beds, the King stopped and repeated his questions. The hermit
again gave no answer, but rose, stretched out his
hand for the spade, and said: "Now rest awhile-
and let me work a bit."

But the King did not give him the spade, and
continued to dig. One hour passed, and another.
The sun began to sink behind the trees, and the
King at last stuck the spade into the ground, and
said: "I came to you, wise man, for an answer to
my questions. If you can give me none, tell me
so, and I will return home."

"Here comes some one running," said the
hermit, "let us see who it is."

The King turned round, and saw a bearded
man come running out of the wood. The man
held his hands pressed against his stomach, and
blood was flowing from under them. When he
reached the King, he fell fainting on the ground
moaning feebly.

The King and the hermit unfastened the
man's clothing. There was a large wound in his
stomach. The King washed it as best he could,
and bandaged it with his handkerchief and with
a towel the hermit had. But the blood would
not stop flowing, and the King again and again
removed the bandage soaked with warm blood,
and washed and rebandaged the wound.

When at last the blood ceased flowing, the
man revived and asked for something to drink.
The King brought fresh water and gave it to
him. Meanwhile the sun had set, and it had become cool.

So the King, with the hermit's help, carried the wounded man into the hut and laid him on the bed.

Lying on the bed the man closed his eyes and was quiet; but the King was so tired with his walk and with the work he had done, that he crouched down on the threshold, and also fell asleep--so soundly that he slept all through the short summer night.

When he awoke in the morning, it was long before he could remember where he was, or who was the strange bearded man lying on the bed and gazing intently at him with shining eyes.

"Forgive me!" said the bearded man in a weak voice, when he saw that the King was awake and was looking at him.

"I do not know you, and have nothing to forgive you for," said the King.

"You do not know me, but I know you. I am that enemy of yours who swore to revenge himself on you, because you executed his brother and seized his property. I knew you had gone alone to see the hermit, and I resolved to kill you on your way back.

"But the day passed and you did not return. So I came out from my ambush to find you, and I came upon your bodyguard, and they recognized me, and wounded me. I escaped from them, but should have bled to death had you not dressed my wound. I wished to kill you, and you have saved my life.

"Now, if I live, and if you wish it, I will serve you as your most faithful slave, and will bid my sons do the same. Forgive me!"

The King was very glad to have made peace with his enemy so easily, and to have gained him for a friend, and he not only forgave him, but said he would send his servants and his own physician to attend him, and promised to restore his property.

Having taken leave of the wounded man, the King went out into the porch and looked around for the hermit. Before going away he wished once more to beg an answer to the questions he had put. The hermit was outside, on his knees, sowing seeds in the beds that had been dug the day before.

The King approached him, and said:

"For the last time, I pray you to answer my questions, wise man."

"You have already been answered!" said the hermit, still crouching on his thin legs, and look-ing up at the King, who stood before him.

"How answered? What do you mean?" asked the King.

"Do you not see," replied the hermit. "If you had not pitied my weakness yesterday, and had not dug those beds for me, but had gone your way, that man would have attacked you, and you would have repented of not having stayed with me.

"So the most important time was when you were digging the beds; and I was the most important man; and to do me good was your most important business.

"Afterwards when that man ran to us, the most important time was when you were attending to him, for if you had not bound up his wounds he would have died without having made peace with you.

"So he was the most important man, and what you did for him was your most important business. Remember then: there is only one time that is important--Now! It is the most important time because it is the only time when we have any power.

"The most necessary man is he with whom you are, for no man knows whether he will ever have dealings with any one else: and the most important affair is, to do him good, because for that purpose alone was man sent into this life!"

사람에겐 얼마만큼의 땅이 필요한가?

HOW MUCH LAND DOES A MAN NEED?

1

An elder sister came to visit her younger
sister in the country. The elder was
married to a tradesman in town, the younger to
a peasant in the village. As the sisters sat over
their tea talking, the elder began to boast of the
advantages of town life: saying how comfortably
they lived there, how well they dressed, what
fine clothes her children wore, what good things
they ate and drank, and how she went to the
theatre, promenades, and entertainments.

The younger sister was piqued, and in turn
disparaged the life of a tradesman, and stood up
for that of a peasant.

"I would not change my way of life for yours," said she. "We may live roughly, but at least we are free from anxiety. You live in better style than we do, but though you often earn more than you need, you are very likely to lose all you have. You know the proverb, 'Loss and gain are brothers twain.' It often happens that people who are wealthy one day are begging their bread the next. Our way is safer. Though a peasant's life is not a fat one, it is a long one. We shall never grow rich, but we shall always have enough to eat."

The elder sister said sneeringly:

"Enough? Yes, if you like to share with the pigs and the calves! What do you know of elegance or manners! However much your good man may slave, you will die as you are living-on a dung heap-and your children the same."

"Well, what of that?" replied the younger. "Of course our work is rough and coarse. But, on the other hand, it is sure; and we need not

bow to any one. But you, in your towns, are sur-
둘러싸다, 에워싸다
rounded by temptations; today all may be right,
유혹, 유혹적인 것
but tomorrow the Evil One may tempt your
악마, 사탄 / 유혹하다, 부추기다
husband with cards, wine, or women, and all
will go to ruin. Don't such things happen often
망치다, 파멸하다 / 자주, 흔히
enough?"

Pahom, the master of the house, was lying
집 주인 / 눕다
on the top of the oven, and he listened to the
오븐, 화덕 / 듣다, 경청하다
women's chatter.
수다, 잡담, 재잘거림
"It is perfectly true," thought he. "Busy as
완전히, 전적으로 / 진실인, 참인 / 바쁜
we are from childhood tilling Mother Earth, we
어린 시절 / 땅을 갈다, 경작하다 / 대지; 지면
peasants have no time to let any nonsense settle
시간이 없는 / 허튼수작, 말도 안 되는 짓
in our heads. Our only trouble is that we haven't
문제, 곤란
land enough. If I had plenty of land, I shouldn't
땅 / 많은
fear the Devil himself!"
악마, 사탄
The women finished their tea, chatted a
마치다, 끝내다 / 수다를 떨다 / 잠시
while about dress, and then cleared away the
~을 치우다
tea-things and lay down to sleep.
찻찬 등의 다과용품
But the Devil had been sitting behind the
~뒤에
oven, and had heard all that was said. He was
오븐, 화덕
pleased that the peasant's wife had led her hus-
기쁘게 하다, 즐겁게 하다 / 소농, 농부 / 아내

band into boasting, and that he had said that
if he had plenty of land he would not fear the
Devil himself.

"All right," thought the Devil. "We will have
a tussle. I'll give you land enough; and by means
of that land I will get you into my power."

2

Close to the village there lived a lady, a small landowner, who had an estate of about three hundred acres.

She had always lived on good terms with the peasants, until she engaged as her steward an old soldier, who took to burdening the people with fines.

However careful Pahom tried to be, it happened again and again that now a horse of his got among the lady's oats, now a cow strayed into her garden, now his calves found their way into her meadows-and he always had to pay a fine.

Pahom paid, but grumbled, and, going home
in a temper, was rough with his family.

All through that summer Pahom had much
trouble because of this steward; and he was
even glad when winter came and the cattle had
to be stabled.

Though he grudged the fodder when they
could no longer graze on the pasture-land, at
least he was free from anxiety about them.

In the winter the news got about that the
lady was going to sell her land, and that the
keeper of the inn on the high road was bargain-
ing for it.

When the peasants heard this they were very
much alarmed.

"Well," thought they, "if the innkeeper gets
the land he will worry us with fines worse than
the lady's steward. We all depend on that estate."

So the peasants went on behalf of their Commune, and asked the lady not to sell the land to

the innkeeper; offering her a better price for it
themselves.

The lady agreed to let them have it. Then the peasants tried to arrange for the Commune to buy the whole estate, so that it might be held by all in common.

They met twice to discuss it, but could not settle the matter; the Evil One sowed discord among them, and they could not agree.

So they decided to buy the land individu- ally, each according to his means; and the lady agreed to this plan as she had to the other.

Presently Pahom heard that a neighbor of his was buying fifty acres, and that the lady had consented to accept one half in cash and to wait a year for the other half. Pahom felt envious.

"Look at that," thought he, "the land is all being sold, and I shall get none of it."

So he spoke to his wife.

"Other people are buying," said he, "and we must also buy twenty acres or so. Life is becom-

ing impossible. That steward is simply crushing
us with his fines."

So they put their heads together and considered how they could manage to buy it. They
had one hundred roubles laid by. They sold a
colt, and one half of their bees; hired out one
of their sons as a laborer, and took his wages in
advance; borrowed the rest from a brother-in-
law, and so scraped together half the purchase
money.

Having done this, Pahom chose out a farm
of forty acres, some of it wooded, and went to
the lady to bargain for it. They came to an agree-
ment, and he shook hands with her upon it, and
paid her a deposit in advance. Then they went
to town and signed the deeds; he paying half the
price down, and undertaking to pay the remain-
der within two years.

So now Pahom had land of his own. He
borrowed seed, and sowed it on the land he had
bought.

The harvest was a good one, and within a
year he had managed to pay off his debts both
to the lady and to his brother-in-law.

So he became a landowner, ploughing and
sowing his own land, making hay on his own
land, cutting his own trees, and feeding his cattle on his own pasture.

When he went out to plough his fields, or to
look at his growing corn, or at his grass meadows, his heart would fill with joy. The grass
that grew and the flowers that bloomed there,
seemed to him unlike any that grew elsewhere.
Formerly, when he had passed by that land, it
had appeared the same as any other land, but
now it seemed quite different.

3

So Pahom was well contented, and everything would have been right if the neighboring peasants would only not have trespassed on his corn-fields and meadows. He appealed to them most civilly, but they still went on: now the Communal herdsmen would let the village cows stray into his meadows; then horses from the night pasture would get among his corn. Pahom turned them out again and again, and forgave their owners, and for a long time he forbore from prosecuting any one. But at last he lost patience and complained to the District Court.

He knew it was the peasants' want of land,
and no evil intent on their part, that caused the
trouble; but he thought:

"I cannot go on overlooking it, or they
will destroy all I have. They must be taught a
lesson."

So he had them up, gave them one lesson,
and then another, and two or three of the peasants were fined. After a time Pahom's neigh-
bours began to bear him a grudge for this, and
would now and then let their cattle on his land
on purpose. One peasant even got into Pahom's
wood at night and cut down five young lime
trees for their bark.

Pahom passing through the wood one day
noticed something white. He came nearer, and
saw the stripped trunks lying on the ground,
and close by stood the stumps, where the tree
had been. Pahom was furious.

"If he had only cut one here and there it
would have been bad enough," thought Pahom,

"but the rascal has actually cut down a whole clump. If I could only find out who did this, I would pay him out."

He racked his brains as to who it could be. Finally he decided: "It must be Simon-no one else could have done it."

So he went to Simon's homestead to have a look around, but he found nothing, and only had an angry scene. However' he now felt more certain than ever that Simon had done it, and he lodged a complaint.

Simon was summoned. The case was tried, and re-tried, and at the end of it all Simon was acquitted, there being no evidence against him. Pahom felt still more aggrieved, and let his anger loose upon the Elder and the Judges.

"You let thieves grease your palms," said he. "If you were honest folk yourselves, you would not let a thief go free."

So Pahom quarrelled with the Judges and with his neighbors.

Threats to burn his building began to be
uttered. So though Pahom had more land, his
place in the Commune was much worse than
before.

About this time a rumor got about that many
people were moving to new parts.

"There's no need for me to leave my land,"
thought Pahom. "But some of the others might
leave our village, and then there would be more
room for us. I would take over their land myself,
and make my estate a bit bigger. I could then
live more at ease. As it is, I am still too cramped
to be comfortable."

One day Pahom was sitting at home, when a
peasant passing through the village, happened
to call in. He was allowed to stay the night, and
supper was given him.

Pahom had a talk with this peasant and
asked him where he came from. The stranger
answered that he came from beyond the Volga,
where he had been working.

One word led to another, and the man went
on to say that many people were settling in
those parts. He told how some people from his
village had settled there. They had joined the
Commune, and had had twenty-five acres per
man granted them.

The land was so good, he said, that the rye
sown on it grew as high as a horse, and so thick
that five cuts of a sickle made a sheaf. One peasant, he said, had brought nothing with him but
his bare hands, and now he had six horses and
two cows of his own.

Pahom's heart kindled with desire. He
thought:

"Why should I suffer in this narrow hole,
if one can live so well elsewhere? I will sell my
land and my homestead here, and with the
money I will start afresh over there and get
everything new. In this crowded place one is always having trouble. But I must first go and find
out all about it myself."

Towards summer he got ready and started. He went down the Volga on a steamer to Samara, then walked another three hundred miles on foot, and at last reached the place. It was just as the stranger had said. The peasants had plenty of land: every man had twenty-five acres of Communal land given him for his use, and any one who had money could buy, besides, at fifty-cents an acre as much good freehold land as he wanted.

Having found out all he wished to know, Pahom returned home as autumn came on, and began selling off his belongings. He sold his land at a profit, sold his homestead and all his cattle, and withdrew from membership of the Commune. He only waited till the spring, and then started with his family for the new settlement.

4

As soon as Pahom and his family arrived at their new abode, he applied for admission into the Commune of a large village. He stood treat to the Elders, and obtained the necessary documents.

Five shares of Communal land were given him for his own and his sons' use: that is to say--125 acres (not altogether, but in different fields) besides the use of the Communal pasture. Pahom put up the buildings he needed, and bought cattle. Of the Communal land alone he had three times as much as at his former home, and the land was good corn-land.

He was ten times better off than he had
been. He had plenty of arable land and pastur-
age, and could keep as many head of cattle as he
liked.

At first, in the bustle of building and settling
down, Pahom was pleased with it all, but when
he got used to it he began to think that even
here he had not enough land.

The first year, he sowed wheat on his share
of the Communal land, and had a good crop.
He wanted to go on sowing wheat, but had not
enough Communal land for the purpose, and
what he had already used was not available; for
in those parts wheat is only sown on virgin soil
or on fallow land.

It is sown for one or two years, and then the
land lies fallow till it is again overgrown with
prairie grass.

There were many who wanted such land,
and there was not enough for all; so that people
quarrelled about it.

Those who were better off, wanted it for growing wheat, and those who were poor, wanted it to let to dealers, so that they might raise money to pay their taxes.

Pahom wanted to sow more wheat; so he rented land from a dealer for a year. He sowed much wheat and had a fine crop, but the land was too far from the village--the wheat had to be carted more than ten miles. After a time Pahom noticed that some peasant-dealers were living on separate farms, and were growing wealthy; and he thought:

"If I were to buy some freehold land, and have a homestead on it, it would be a different thing, altogether. Then it would all be nice and compact."

The question of buying freehold land recurred to him again and again.

He went on in the same way for three years; renting land and sowing wheat. The seasons turned out well and the crops were good, so that

he began to lay money by. He might have gone
돈을 저축하다[모으다]
on living contentedly, but he grew tired of hav-
흡족하게, 만족스럽게   지치다, 싫증나다
ing to rent other people's land every year, and
빌리다, 세내다   매~ 각~
having to scramble for it. Wherever there was
(여러 사람이 경쟁하듯) 서로 밀치다[앞다투다]
good land to be had, the peasants would rush
달려들다
for it and it was taken up at once, so that unless
즉시, 당장   ~아니면
you were sharp about it you got none.
영리한, 약삭빠른

It happened in the third year that he and a
~이 일어나다[발생하다]
dealer together rented a piece of pasture land
빌리다   조각   초원, 목초지
from some peasants; and they had already
이미, 벌써
ploughed it up, when there was some dispute,
경작하다, 밭을 갈다   이의를 제기하다
and the peasants went to law about it, and
법
things fell out so that the labor was all lost.
떨어져 나가다   노동, 근로   잃다, 빼앗기다

"If it were my own land," thought Pahom, "I

should be independent, and there would not be
독립적인, 독자적인
all this unpleasantness."
악감정, 불화, 불쾌함

So Pahom began looking out for land which
~을 찾다
he could buy; and he came across a peasant who
우연히 만나다[마주치다]
had bought thirteen hundred acres, but hav-
사다   1,300에이커
ing got into difficulties was willing to sell again
어려움, 곤란   기꺼이 ~하다   팔다
cheap.
싸게

Pahom bargained and haggled with him, and

협상[흥정]하다　(물건 값을 두고) 실랑이를 벌이다, 흥정하다

at last they settled the price at 1,500 roubles,

합의를 보다, 결정하다

part in cash and part to be paid later.

현금으로　나중에, 뒤에

They had all but clinched the matter, when a

매듭짓다, 결말을 내다

passing dealer happened to stop at Pahom's one

지나가는　(어떤 일이) ~에게 일어나다[생기다], …게 되다

day to get a feed for his horse. He drank tea with

마시다

Pahom, and they had a talk.

The dealer said that he was just returning

지금 막, 바로, 딱

from the land of the Bashkirs, far away, where

멀리 떨어진, 먼(=distant)

he had bought thirteen thousand acres of land

13　1,000

all for 1,000 roubles. Pahom questioned him

질문하다

further, and the tradesman said:

더 이상의, 추가의

"All one need do is to make friends with the

친구가 되다

chiefs. I gave away about one hundred roubles'

(단체의) 최고위자[장]

worth of dressing-gowns and carpets, besides a

…의 가치가 있는[되는]　게다가, 뿐만 아니라

case of tea, and I gave wine to those who would

와인, 포도주

drink it; and I got the land for less than two

…보다 적은

cents an acre. And he showed Pahom the title-

부동산 권리증서

deeds, saying:

"The land lies near a river, and the whole

가까이, 근처에　전부, 전체의

prairie is virgin soil."

대초원　처녀지

Pahom plied him with questions, and the tradesman said:

"There is more land there than you could cover if you walked a year, and it all belongs to the Bashkirs. They are as simple as sheep, and land can be got almost for nothing."

"There now," thought Pahom, "with my one thousand roubles, why should I get only thirteen hundred acres, and saddle myself with a debt besides. If I take it out there, I can get more than ten times as much for the money."

5

Pahom inquired how to get to the place, and as soon as the tradesman had left him, he prepared to go there himself. He left his wife to look after the homestead, and started on his journey taking his man with him.

They stopped at a town on their way, and bought a case of tea, some wine, and other presents, as the tradesman had advised.

On and on they went until they had gone more than three hundred miles, and on the seventh day they came to a place where the Bashkirs had pitched their tents. It was all just as the tradesman had said.

The people lived on the steppes (스텝 지대), by a river, in felt-covered tents. They neither tilled (~도 아니고 ~도 아닌) the ground, nor ate bread (먹다 / 빵). Their cattle (소) and horses (말) grazed in herds on the steppe (방목하다, 놓아먹이다).

The colts (수망아지) were tethered ((동물이 멀리 가지 못하게 말뚝에) 묶다) behind the tents, and the mares (암말, 암당나귀) were driven to them (몰고 가다) twice a day (2번). The mares were milked (젖을 짜다), and from the milk kumiss (쿠미스(말의 젖을 원료로 하여 만든 술)) was made.

It was the women (여자, 부인) who prepared kumiss, and they also (또한, 역시) made cheese (치즈). As far as the men were (…하는 한, …에 관한 한) concerned, drinking kumiss and tea, eating (~에 흥미[관심]를 갖다) mutton (양고기), and playing on their pipes (피리), was all they cared about (…에 마음을 쓰다, …에 관심을 가지다). They were all stout (통통한, 튼튼한) and merry (즐거운, 쾌활한), and all the summer (여름) long they never thought of doing any work. They were quite (상당히, 꽤) ignorant (무식한, 무지한), and knew no Russian (러시아 어), but were good-natured (온화한, 부드러운, 성격 좋은) enough.

As soon as they saw Pahom, they came out of their tents and gathered (모으다) round (둥글게) their visitor (방문객, 손님). An interpreter (통역사) was found, and Pahom told them he had come about some land.

The Bashkirs seemed very glad (기쁜, 반가운); they took

Pahom and led him into one of the best tents, where they made him sit on some down cushions placed on a carpet, while they sat round him.

They gave him tea and kumiss, and had a sheep killed, and gave him mutton to eat. Pahom took presents out of his cart and distributed them among the Bashkirs, and divided amongst them the tea. The Bashkirs were delighted. They talked a great deal among themselves, and then told the interpreter to translate.

"They wish to tell you," said the interpreter, "that they like you, and that it is our custom to do all we can to please a guest and to repay him for his gifts. You have given us presents, now tell us which of the things we possess please you best, that we may present them to you."

"What pleases me best here," answered Pahom, "is your land. Our land is crowded, and the soil is exhausted; but you have plenty of land and it is good land. I never saw the like of it."

The interpreter translated. The Bashkirs talked among themselves for a while. Pahom could not understand what they were saying, but saw that they were much amused, and that they shouted and laughed. Then they were silent and looked at Pahom while the interpreter said:

"They wish me to tell you that in return for your presents they will gladly give you as much land as you want. You have only to point it out with your hand and it is yours."

The Bashkirs talked again for a while and began to dispute. Pahom asked what they were disputing about, and the interpreter told him that some of them thought they ought to ask their Chief about the land and not act in his ab-sence, while others thought there was no need to wait for his return.

6

While the Bashkirs were disputing, a man in a large fox-fur cap appeared on the scene. They all became silent and rose to their feet. The interpreter said, "This is our Chief himself."

Pahom immediately fetched the best dressing-gown and five pounds of tea, and offered these to the Chief. The Chief accepted them, and seated himself in the place of honour. The Bashkirs at once began telling him something. The Chief listened for a while, then made a sign with his head for them to be silent, and addressing himself to Pahom, said in Russian:

"Well, let it be so. Choose whatever piece of land you like; we have plenty of it."

"How can I take as much as I like?" thought Pahom. "I must get a deed to make it secure, or else they may say, 'It is yours,' and afterwards may take it away again."

"Thank you for your kind words," he said aloud. "You have much land, and I only want a little. But I should like to be sure which bit is mine. Could it not be measured and made over to me? Life and death are in God's hands. You good people give it to me, but your children might wish to take it away again."

"You are quite right," said the Chief. "We will make it over to you."

"I heard that a dealer had been here," continued Pahom, "and that you gave him a little land, too, and signed title-deeds to that effect. I should like to have it done in the same way."

The Chief understood.

"Yes," replied he, "that can be done quite

easily. We have a scribe, and we will go to town
with you and have the deed properly sealed."

"And what will be the price?" asked Pahom.

"Our price is always the same: one thousand
roubles a day."

"A day? What measure is that? How many
acres would that be?"

"We do not know how to reckon it out," said
the Chief. "We sell it by the day. As much as you
can go round on your feet in a day is yours, and
the price is one thousand roubles a day."

Pahom was surprised.

"But in a day you can get round a large tract
of land," he said.

The Chief laughed.

"It will all be yours!" said he. "But there is
one condition: If you don't return on the same
day to the spot whence you started, your money
is lost."

"But how am I to mark the way that I have
gone?"

"Why, we shall go to any spot you like, and stay there. You must start from that spot and make your round, taking a spade with you. Wherever you think necessary, make a mark. At every turning, dig a hole and pile up the turf; then afterwards we will go round with a plough from hole to hole. You may make as large a circuit as you please, but before the sun sets you must return to the place you started from. All the land you cover will be yours."

Pahom was delighted. It was decided to start early next morning. They talked a while, and after drinking some more kumiss and eating some more mutton, they had tea again, and then the night came on. They gave Pahom a feather-bed to sleep on, and the Bashkirs dispersed for the night, promising to assemble the next morning at daybreak and ride out before sunrise to the appointed spot.

7

Pahom lay on the feather-bed, but could not sleep. He kept thinking about the land.

"What a large tract I will mark off!" thought he. "I can easily go thirty-five miles in a day. The days are long now, and within a circuit of thirty-five miles what a lot of land there will be! I will sell the poorer land, or let it to peasants, but I'll pick out the best and farm it. I will buy two ox-teams, and hire two more laborers. About a hundred and fifty acres shall be plough-land, and I will pasture cattle on the rest."

Pahom lay awake all night, and dozed off only just before dawn. Hardly were his eyes

closed when he had a dream. He thought he was
lying in that same tent, and heard somebody
chuckling outside. He wondered who it could be,
and rose and went out, and he saw the Bashkir
Chief sitting in front of the tent holding his side
and rolling about with laughter. Going nearer to
the Chief, Pahom asked: "What are you laughing
at?"

But he saw that it was no longer the Chief,
but the dealer who had recently stopped at his
house and had told him about the land. Just as
Pahom was going to ask, "Have you been here
long?"

He saw that it was not the dealer, but the
peasant who had come up from the Volga, long
ago, to Pahom's old home. Then he saw that it
was not the peasant either, but the Devil himself with hoofs and horns, sitting there and
chuckling, and before him lay a man barefoot,
prostrate on the ground, with only trousers and
a shirt on.

And Pahom dreamt that he looked more attentively to see what sort of a man it was lying there, and he saw that the man was dead, and that it was himself! He awoke horror-struck.

"What things one does dream," thought he.

Looking round he saw through the open door that the dawn was breaking.

"It's time to wake them up," thought he. "We ought to be starting."

He got up, roused his man (who was sleeping in his cart), bade him harness; and went to call the Bashkirs.

"It's time to go to the steppe to measure the land," he said.

The Bashkirs rose and assembled, and the Chief came, too. Then they began drinking kumiss again, and offered Pahom some tea, but he would not wait.

"If we are to go, let us go. It is high time," said he.

8

The Bashkirs got ready and they all started:
some mounted on horses, and some in
carts. Pahom drove in his own small cart with
his servant, and took a spade with him. When
they reached the steppe, the morning red was
beginning to kindle. They ascended a hillock
(called by the Bashkirs a shikhan) and dismount-
ing from their carts and their horses, gathered
in one spot. The Chief came up to Pahom and
stretched out his arm towards the plain:

"See," said he, "all this, as far as your eye can
reach, is ours. You may have any part of it you
like."

Pahom's eyes glistened: it was all virgin soil,
반짝이다, 번들거리다 　　　　　　미개간지, 처녀지
as flat as the palm of your hand, as black as the
평평한, 평지인　손바닥
seed of a poppy, and in the hollows different
씨앗, 씨　　　양귀비　　　　　　　(땅 속으로) 움푹 꺼진 곳
kinds of grasses grew breast high.
(가축 먹이용) 풀[꼴], 잔디　가슴 높이로

The Chief took off his fox-fur cap, placed it
~을 벗다　　　　　　　　　　　　놓다, 두다
on the ground and said:

"This will be the mark. Start from here, and
표시
return here again. All the land you go round
돌아오다
shall be yours."

Pahom took out his money and put it on the
~을 꺼내다　　　　돈
cap. Then he took off his outer coat, remaining
외투　　　남아 있는
in his sleeveless under coat. He unfastened his
소매 없는　　　　　　　　　풀다
girdle and tied it tight below his stomach, put
거들, 띠, 허리띠　묶다　단단히, 꽉　아래[밑]에　배
a little bag of bread into the breast of his coat,
(옷의) 가슴 (부분)
and tying a flask of water to his girdle, he drew
묶다　휴대용 물병　　　　　　　　끌어당기다
up the tops of his boots, took the spade from his
삽, 가래
man, and stood ready to start. He considered for
숙고하다, 고려하다
some moments which way he had better go--it
잠깐, 순간　　　　　　길
was tempting everywhere.
유혹하다, 부추기다
"No matter," he concluded, "I will go to-
결론[판단]을 내리다
wards the rising sun."

He turned his face to the east, stretched himself, and waited for the sun to appear above the rim.

"I must lose no time," he thought, "and it is easier walking while it is still cool."

The sun's rays had hardly flashed above the horizon, before Pahom, carrying the spade over his shoulder, went down into the steppe.

Pahom started walking neither slowly nor quickly. After having gone a thousand yards he stopped, dug a hole and placed pieces of turf one on another to make it more visible. Then he went on; and now that he had walked off his stiffness he quickened his pace. After a while he dug another hole.

Pahom looked back. The hillock could be distinctly seen in the sunlight, with the people on it, and the glittering tires of the cartwheels. At a rough guess Pahom concluded that he had walked three miles. It was growing warmer; he took off his under-coat, flung it across his shoulder, and went on again. It had grown quite warm now; he looked at the sun, it was time to think of breakfast.

"The first shift is done, but there are four in a day, and it is too soon yet to turn. But I will just take off my boots," said he to himself.

He sat down, took off his boots, stuck them into his girdle, and went on. It was easy walking now.

"I will go on for another three miles," thought he, "and then turn to the left. The spot is so fine, that it would be a pity to lose it. The further one goes, the better the land seems."

He went straight on a for a while, and when he looked round, the hillock was scarcely visible and the people on it looked like black ants, and he could just see something glistening there in the sun.

"Ah," thought Pahom, "I have gone far enough in this direction, it is time to turn. Besides I am in a regular sweat, and very thirsty."

He stopped, dug a large hole, and heaped
파다 쌓아 올리다
up pieces of turf. Next he untied his flask, had
잔디, 떼 풀다 물병
a drink, and then turned sharply to the left. He
급격히 왼쪽
went on and on; the grass was high, and it was
계속해서 가다 풀 높은
very hot.
더운, 뜨거운

Pahom began to grow tired: he looked at the
피곤한, 지친
sun and saw that it was noon.
정오, 낮 12시

"Well," he thought, "I must have a rest."
쉬다, 휴식하다

He sat down, and ate some bread and drank
앉다 먹다 빵 마시다
some water; but he did not lie down, thinking
물 바닥에 눕다
that if he did he might fall asleep. After sitting a
잠 들다
little while, he went on again. At first he walked
처음에는
easily: the food had strengthened him; but it
쉽게, 쉽사리, 용이하게 강화하다
had become terribly hot, and he felt sleepy; still
끔찍하게, 혹독하게 졸린, 잠이 오는
he went on, thinking: "An hour to suffer, a life-
시달리다, 고통을 받다
time to live."

He went a long way in this direction also,
방향, 쪽 역시
and was about to turn to the left again, when he
perceived a damp hollow: "It would be a pity to
감지하다 축축한 (땅 속으로) 움푹 꺼진 곳 유감, 애석함
leave that out," he thought. "Flax would do well
아마 (섬유)
there."

120

So he went on past the hollow, and dug a
hole on the other side of it before he turned the
corner. Pahom looked towards the hillock. The
heat made the air hazy: it seemed to be quiver-
ing, and through the haze the people on the hillock could scarcely be seen.

"Ah!" thought Pahom, "I have made the
sides too long; I must make this one shorter."
And he went along the third side, stepping
faster. He looked at the sun: it was nearly half
way to the horizon, and he had not yet done two
miles of the third side of the square. He was still
ten miles from the goal.

"No," he thought, "though it will make my
land lopsided, I must hurry back in a straight
line now. I might go too far, and as it is I have a
great deal of land."

So Pahom hurriedly dug a hole, and turned
straight towards the hillock.

9

Pahom went straight towards the hillock,
but he now walked with difficulty. He was
done up with the heat, his bare feet were cut
and bruised, and his legs began to fail.
He longed to rest, but it was impossible if he
meant to get back before sunset. The sun waits
for no man, and it was sinking lower and lower.

"Oh dear," he thought, "if only I have not
blundered trying for too much! What if I am too
late?"

He looked towards the hillock and at the
sun. He was still far from his goal, and the sun
was already near the rim.

Pahom walked on and on; it was very hard
힘든, 어려운
walking, but he went quicker and quicker. He
점점 더 빨리
pressed on, but was still far from the place. He
분발하다, 뛰다, 재촉하다
began running, threw away his coat, his boots,
내팽개치다
his flask, and his cap, and kept only the spade
삽, 가래
which he used as a support.
버팀대, 지지대
"What shall I do," he thought again, "I have
grasped too much, and ruined the whole affair. I
욕심 부리다   망치다, 파멸하다
can't get there before the sun sets."

And this fear made him still more breath-
공포, 두려움   더욱 숨이 가쁜[숨 막히는]
less. Pahom went on running, his soaking shirt
완전히 다 젖은, 흠뻑 젖은
and trousers stuck to him, and his mouth was
parched. His breast was working like a black-
바싹 마르게[몹시 건조하게] 하다   대장장이
smith's bellows, his heart was beating like a
풀무   심장   세게 치다[두드리다]
hammer, and his legs were giving way as if they
망치   다리   무릎이 꺾이다
did not belong to him. Pahom was seized with
~에 속한   꽉 붙잡다
terror lest he should die of the strain.
공포, 두려움   부담, 중압[압박](감)
Though afraid of death, he could not stop.
비록 ~지만   ~을 두려워하다
"After having run all that way they will call
me a fool if I stop now," thought he.
바보, 멍청이
And he ran on and on, and drew near and

heard the Bashkirs yelling and shouting to him,
and their cries inflamed his heart still more. He
gathered his last strength and ran on.

The sun was close to the rim, and cloaked in
mist looked large, and red as blood.

Now, yes now, it was about to set! The sun
was quite low, but he was also quite near his
aim.

Pahom could already see the people on the
hillock waving their arms to hurry him up.
He could see the fox-fur cap on the ground,
and the money on it, and the Chief sitting on the
ground holding his sides. And Pahom remembered his dream.

"There is plenty of land," thought he, "but
will God let me live on it? I have lost my life, I
have lost my life! I shall never reach that spot!"
Pahom looked at the sun, which had reached
the earth: one side of it had already disappeared.
With all his remaining strength he rushed on,
bending his body forward so that his legs could

hardly follow fast enough to keep him from falling. Just as he reached the hillock it suddenly
grew dark. He looked up--the sun had already
set. He gave a cry:

"All my labor has been in vain," thought he,
and was about to stop, but he heard the Bashkirs still shouting, and remembered that though
to him, from below, the sun seemed to have set,
they on the hillock could still see it. He took a
long breath and ran up the hillock.

It was still light there. He reached the top
and saw the cap. Before it sat the Chief laughing and holding his sides. Again Pahom remembered his dream, and he uttered a cry: his
legs gave way beneath him, he fell forward and
reached the cap with his hands.

"Ah, what a fine fellow!" exclaimed the Chief.
"He has gained much land!"
Pahom's servant came running up and tried
to raise him, but he saw that blood was flowing
from his mouth. Pahom was dead!

The Bashkirs clicked their tongues to show
혀를 끌끌 차다
their pity.
유감, 애석함, 동정
His servant picked up the spade and dug a
집어들다   삽, 가래   파다
grave long enough for Pahom to lie in, and bur-
무덤, 묘(tomb)   묻다
ied him in it. Six feet from his head to his heels
머리에서 발끝까지
was all he needed.

바보 이반

IVAN THE FOOL

1

Once upon a time there lived a rich peasant,
옛날 옛적에, 옛날에   부유한   농부
who had three sons—Simon the Warrior,
          3   아들   전사, 군인
Taras the Pot-bellied, and Ivan the Fool, and a
          배가 불룩한   바보, 멍청이
deaf and dumb daughter, Malania, an old maid.
농아의, 농아자의   딸   노처녀
Simon the Warrior went off to the wars to
                                        전쟁
serve the King; Taras the Pot-bellied went to a
섬기다   왕
merchant's to trade in the town, and Ivan the
상인, 무역상   거래[교역/무역]하다   (소)도시, 읍
Fool and the old maid stayed at home to do the
                              머물다
work of the house and the farm.
                              농장
Simon the Warrior earned a high rank for
                    벌다, 얻다, 받다   고위직
himself and an estate and married a nobleman's
              (대규모) 사유지[토지]   귀족
daughter. He had a large income and a large es-
                          소득, 수입
tate, but he could never make both ends meet,

for, what he managed to gather in, his wife managed to squander; thus it was that he never had any money.

And Simon the Warrior went to his estate one day to collect his income, and his steward said to him, "There is nothing to squeeze money out of; we have neither cattle, nor implements, nor horses, nor cows, nor ploughs, nor harrows; we must get all these things first, then there will be an income."

Then Simon the Warrior went to his father and said, "You are rich, father; and have given me nothing, let me have a third of your posses-sions and I will set up my estate."

And the old man replied, "Why should I? You have brought nothing to the home. It would be unfair to Ivan and the girl."

And Simon said, "Ivan is a fool and Malania is deaf and dumb; they do not need much, sure-ly."

"Ivan shall decide," the old man said.

And Ivan said, "I don't mind; let him take what he wants."

Simon took a portion of his father's goods and moved them to his estate, and once more he set out to serve the King.

Taras the Pot-bellied made a great deal of money and married a merchant's widow, but still, it seemed to him that he had not enough, so he too went to his father and said, "Give me my portion, father."

And the old man was loath to give Taras his portion, and he said, "You have brought us nothing; everything in the home has been earned by Ivan; it would be unfair to him and the girl."

And Taras said, "Ivan is a fool, what does he need? He cannot marry, for no one would have him, and the girl is deaf and dumb and does not need much either."

And turning to Ivan, he said, "Let me have half the corn, Ivan. I will not take any imple-

ments, and as for the cattle, I only want the grey
cob; he is of no use to you for the plough."

Ivan laughed.

"Very well," he said, "you shall have what
you want."

And Taras was given his portion, and he
carted the corn off to the town and took away
the grey cob, and Ivan was left with only the old
mare to work the farm and support his father
and mother.

2

The old Devil was annoyed that the three
brothers had not quarrelled over the matter and had parted in peace. He summoned
three little Devilkins.

"There are three brothers," he said, "Simon
the Warrior, Taras the Pot-bellied, and Ivan the
Fool. I want them all to quarrel and they live in
peace and goodwill. It is the Fool's fault. Go to
these three brothers, the three of you, and con-
found them so that they will scratch out each
others' eyes. Do you think you can do it?"

"We can," they said.

"How will you do it?"

"We will ruin them first," they said, "so that they have nothing to eat, then we will put them all together and they will begin to fight."

"I see you know your work," the old Devil said. "Go then, and do not return to me until you have confounded the whole three, or else I will skin you alive."

And the Devilkins set out to a bog to confer on the matter, and they argued and argued, for each wanted the easiest work, and they decided to cast lots and each to take the brother that fell to him, and whichever finished his work first was to help the others.

And the Devilkins cast lots and fixed a day when they should meet again in the bog, in order to find out who had finished his work and who was in need of help.

The day arrived and the Devilkins gathered together in the bog. They began to discuss their work. The first to give his account was the one who had undertaken Simon the Warrior.

"My work is progressing well," he said. "To-morrow Simon will return to his father."

"How did you manage it?" the others asked him.

"First of all," he said, "I gave Simon so much courage that he promised the King to conquer the whole world. And the King made him the head of his army and sent him to make war on the King of India. That same night I damped the powder of Simon's troops and I went to the King of India and made him numberless soldiers out of straw.

"And when Simon saw himself surrounded by the straw soldiers, a fear came upon him and he ordered the guns to fire, but the guns and cannon would not go off. And Simon's troops were terrified and ran away like sheep, and the King of India defeated them.

"Simon was disgraced. He was deprived of his rank and estate and to-morrow he is to be executed.

134

"I have only one day left in which to get him out of the dungeon and help him to escape home. To-morrow I shall have finished with him, so I want you to tell me which of you two is in need of help."

Then the second Devilkin began to tell of his work with Taras.

"I do not want help," he said; "my work is also going well. Taras will not live in the town another week. The first thing I did was to make his belly grow bigger and fill him with greed. He is now so greedy for other people's goods that whatever he sees he must buy. He has bought up everything he could lay his eyes on, and spent all his money, and is still buying with borrowed money. He has taken so much upon himself, and become so entangled that he will never pull himself out. In a week he will have to repay the borrowed money, and I will turn his wares into manure so that he cannot repay, then he will go to his father."

"And how is your work getting on?" they asked the third Devilkin about Ivan.

"My work is going badly," he said. "The first thing I did was to spit into Ivan's jug of kvas to give him a stomach-ache and then I went into his fields and made the soil as hard as stones so that he could not move it.

"I thought he would not plough it, but the fool came with his plough and began to pull. His stomach-ache made him groan, yet still he went on ploughing.

"I broke one plough for him and he went home and repaired another, and again persisted in his work. I crawled beneath the ground and clutched hold of his ploughshares, but I could not hold them—he pressed upon the plough so hard, and the shares were sharp and cut my hands. He has finished it all but one strip.

"You must come and help me, mates, for singly we shall never get the better of him, and all our labour will be wasted.

"If the fool keeps on tilling his land, the
other two brothers will never know what need
means, for he will feed them."

The first Devilkin offered to come and help
to-morrow when he had disposed of Simon the
Warrior, and with that the three Devilkins parted.

3

Ivan had ploughed all the fallow but one
strip, and he went to finish that. His stomach
ached, yet he had to plough. He undid the harness ropes, turned over the plough and set out
to the fields. He drove one furrow, but coming
back, the ploughshares caught on something
that seemed like a root.

"What a strange thing!" Ivan thought. "There
were no roots here, yet here's a root!"

He put his hand into the furrow and clutched
hold of something soft. He pulled it out. It was a
thing as black as a root and it moved. He looked
closely and saw that it was a live Devilkin.

갈다, 경작하다 / 휴한지 / 고랑 / 끝내다, 마치다 / 배 / 아픈 / (묶인 것을) 풀다 / 마구 / 쟁기 / 출발하다 / (쟁기질로 생긴) 고랑[골] / 쟁기날 / 잡다, 붙잡다 / 뿌리 / 이상한, 기이한 / 뿌리 / 여기, 이곳 / 고랑, 골 / 꽉 붙잡다 / 부드러운 / 잡아당겨 꺼내다 / 검은, 까만 / 움직이다 / 가까이, 자세히 / 소악마, 작은 악마

"You horrid little wretch, you!"

Ivan raised his hand to dash its head against the plough, but the Devilkin squealed, "Don't kill me, and I'll do whatever you want me to."

"What can you do?"

"Tell me what you want."

Ivan scratched his head.

"My stomach aches," he said; "can you make it well?"

"I can."

"Do it, then."

The Devilkin bent down, rummaged about with his nails in the furrow and pulled out three little roots, grown together.

"There," he said; "if any one swallows a single one of these roots all pain will pass away from him."

Ivan took the three roots, separated them and swallowed one. His stomach-ache instantly left him.

"Let me go now," the Devilkin begged once

more. "I will dive through the earth and never bother you again."

"Very well," Ivan said; "go, in God's name."

At the mention of God the Devilkin plunged into the ground like a stone thrown into water, and there was nothing but the hole left.

Ivan thrust the two remaining little roots into his cap and went on with his ploughing. He finished the strip, turned over his plough and set off home.

He unharnessed and went into the house, and there was his brother, Simon the Warrior, sitting at table with his wife, having supper. His estate had been taken from him; he had escaped from prison and come back to live with his father.

As soon as Simon the Warrior saw Ivan, he said to him, "I have come with my wife to live with you; will you keep us both until I find another place?"

"Very well," Ivan said, "you can live here."

When Ivan sat down by the table, the smell of him was displeasing to the lady and she said to her husband, "I cannot sup together with a stinking peasant."

And Simon the Warrior said, "My lady says you do not smell sweet; you had better eat in the passage."

"Very well," Ivan said. "It is time for bed anyway, and I must feed the mare."

Ivan took some bread and his coat and went out for the night.

4

That night, having freed himself of Simon the Warrior, the first little Devilkin set out to seek Ivan's Devilkin, to help him plague the Fool as they had agreed. He came to the fields, looked all round for his mate, but he was nowhere to be seen; he only found a hole.

"I see some misfortune has happened to my mate; I must take his place. The ploughing is all finished; I must upset the Fool at the mowing."

And the Devilkin went to the meadow and flooded it and trampled the hay in the mud.

Ivan awoke at daybreak, put his scythe in order and set out to the meadow to mow the hay.

Ivan swung the scythe once, he swung it
휙 움직이다(swing)
twice, but the scythe grew blunt and would not
2번 　　　　　　　　　　　　　무딘, 뭉툭한
cut; he had to sharpen it. Ivan struggled and
　　　　　　날카롭게 하다　　　　　투쟁[고투]하다, 애쓰다
struggled and struggled.

"This won't do," he said; "I must go home
and bring a whetstone and a hunk of bread.
가져오다　　숫돌　　　　　　　빵 한 덩어리
If it takes me a week. I'll not give up until I've
　　　　　　　　　　　　　　포기하다, 그만두다
mowed it every bit."
(풀 등을) 베다
And the Devilkin grew pensive when he
　　　　　　　　　　　깊은 생각[수심]에 잠긴, 수심 어린
heard these words. "The Fool has a temper," he
　　　　　　　　　　　　　　　　　성질, 성미
said; "I can't catch him this way; I must think of
　　　　　　잡다　　　　　　　방법, 방식
something else."
또[그 밖의] 다른
Ivan returned, sharpened his scythe and be-
올아오다　　　날카롭게 하다　　큰 낫
gan to mow. The Devilkin crept into the grass,
　　　　　　　　　　　살살 기어가다(creep)
caught hold of the scythe by the heel and pushed
　　　　　　　　　　　　발뒤꿈치　　밀다
the point into the ground. It was hard for Ivan,
(사물의 뾰족한) 끝　　　　　　어려운, 힘든
but he mowed all the grass, except a little piece
풀을 베다　　　　　　　~를 제외한, ~만 빼고
in the swamp.
늪, 습지
The Devilkin crept into the swamp, thinking,
　　　　　　　　　　　　　늪, 습지
"Even if I have to cut my hands I won't let him
(비록) …일지라도, (설사) …이라고 할지라도
mow that!"

143

Ivan came to the swamp. The grass was not
늪지, 숲지
thick, but the scythe could not cut through it.
빽빽한   큰 낫
Ivan grew angry and began to mow with all his
점점 화가 나다   있는 힘을 다하여
might.

The Devilkin began to lose hold, seeing that
시작하다   잃다, 상실하다
he was in a bad plight, but he had no time to get
역경, 곤경
away and took refuge in a bush.
피난(처), 피신(처), 도피(처)
Ivan swung the scythe near the bush and cut
휘두르다   큰 낫   가까운, 근처의   관목숲, 덤불
off half the Devilkin's tail. He finished mowing
반, 절반   꼬리   마치다   풀 베다
the grass, told the old maid to rake it up and
노처녀   갈퀴로 모으다
went away to mow the rye.
호밀
He came to the field with his sickle, but the
낫
Devilkin with the clipped tail was there before
잘린   먼저, 앞서
him. He had entangled the rye, so that the sickle
엮어매다, 헝클어뜨리다   낫
could not take it. Ivan went back for his reaping-
낫(곡식 수확용)
hook and reaped the whole field of rye.
(농작물을) 수확하다[거둬들이다]
"Now," he said, "I must tackle the oats."
씨름하다   귀리
At these words the Devilkin with the clipped
잘린
tail thought, "I did not trip him up with the rye,
다리를 걸어서 거꾸러뜨리다
but I'll do so with the oats. If only the morrow
귀리
would come!"

In the morning the Devilkin hurried off to the field of oats, but the oats were all harvested. Ivan had reaped them overnight so that less of the grain should be wasted. The Devilkin lost his temper at that.

"He has mutilated and exhausted me, the fool! I've never had such trouble on the battle-field even. The wretch doesn't sleep and you can't get ahead of him. I'll creep into the stacks of sheaves and rot the grain."

And the Devilkin crept into a stack of sheaves, and began to rot them. He heated them, grew warm himself and fell asleep.

Ivan harnessed the mare and set out with his sister to gather in the sheaves. He stopped by the stack and began to throw the sheaves into the cart. He had thrown up two sheaves and was going to take up a third, when the fork dug into the Devilkin's back. He looked at the prongs and saw a live Devilkin with his tail clipped, wrig-gling and writhing and trying to get away.

"You horrid little wretch! You here again!"

"I'm not the same one," the Devilkin pleaded. "The other was my brother. I belong to your brother Simon."

"Whoever you are you shall share the same fate."

Ivan was about to dash it against the cart, when the Devilkin cried out, "Spare me! I'll not worry you again, and I'll do whatever you want me to."

"What can you do?"

"I can make soldiers out of anything you choose."

"What good are they?"

"You can make them do anything you like. Soldiers can do everything."

"Can they play songs?"

"They can."

"Very well; make some, then."

And the Devilkin said, "Take a sheaf of rye and bump it upright on the ground, saying,—

My slave bids you be a sheaf no more.
노예　명령하다, 분부를 내리다

Every straw contained in you,
밀짚, 지푸라기　포함하다

Must turn into a soldier true."
변하다　군인

Ivan took the sheaf and banged it on the
단, 묶음　쾅[탕]하고 치다[때리다]
ground and repeated the Devilkin's words. And
반복하다, 되풀이하다
the sheaf burst asunder and every straw turned
터지다　산산이, 뿔뿔이　~로 변하다
into a soldier and at their head the drummer
(북을 치는) 고수
and bugler were playing. Ivan laughed aloud.
나팔수　큰소리로

"That was clever of you," he said. "It will
영리한, 똑똑한, 기발한, 재치 있는
amuse Malania."
즐겁게[미소 짓게/재미있게] 하다

"Let me go now," the Devilkin begged.
애원하다

"Not yet," Ivan said. "I shall want to make
the soldiers out of chaff so as not to waste the
왕겨, 여물　낭비하다
grain. Show me first how to turn the soldiers
곡식
into a sheaf again, so that I can thresh it."
타작[탈곡]하다

And the Devilkin said, "Repeat the words—
되풀이하다, 반복하다

My slave bids every soldier be a straw
노예　명하다　군인　짚
And turn into a sheaf once more."
묶음, 단

147

Ivan repeated the Devilkin's words, and the soldiers turned into a sheaf again.

And again the Devilkin pleaded, "Let me go."

"Very well," Ivan said, taking him off the prongs. "Go, in God's name."

At the mention of God the Devilkin plunged into the ground like a stone thrown into water, and there was nothing but the hole left.

When Ivan reached home, his other brother, Taras, and his wife were sitting at table and having supper. Taras could not pay his debts; he fled from his creditors and came home to his father.

As soon as he saw Ivan he said, "Until I can make some more money, will you keep me and my wife?"

"Very well," Ivan said. "You can live here."

Ivan took off his coat and sat down to table.

And Taras' wife said, "I cannot sup with a fool; he smells of sweat."

Taras the Pot-bellied said, "You do not smell sweet, Ivan; go and eat in the passage."
복도, 통로

"Very well," Ivan said; "it's time for bed, any-how, and I must feed the mare."

He took his coat and a piece of bread, and
빵 한 조각
went out.

5

That night, having disposed of Taras, the third little Devilkin came to help his mates plague Ivan, as they had agreed.

He came to the ploughed field and looked and looked, but could see no one; he only found the hole.

Then he went to the meadow and found a piece of tail in the swamp, and in the rye-stubble field he found another hole.

"I see some misfortune has happened to my mates. I must take their places and tackle the Fool."

The Devilkin set out to find Ivan.

Ivan had finished his work in the fields and
끝내다, 마치다   일, 작업
had gone into the copse to cut wood.
잡목림, 풀숲

The brothers found it too crowded to live to-
너무나 ~해서 ~할 수 없다
gether in their father's house and they ordered
명령하다, 시키다
Ivan to fell timber to build themselves new
목재, 재목
houses.

The Devilkin rushed into the wood and crept
달려들다, 돌진하다   (살살) 기다
into the knots of the trees to prevent Ivan from
옹이   (~가 ~하는 것을) 막다[예방/방지하다]
felling them.

Ivan had cut a tree in the right way so that
나무를 베다
it should fall on to a clear space, but the tree
넘어지다, 쓰러지다   빈 공간
seemed to be possessed, and fell over where it
(이상한 짓을 하도록) 홀리다
was not wanted, and got entangled among the
엉키다, 얽히다
branches.
나뭇가지
Ivan lopped them off with his bill-hook and
(나무·나뭇가지를) 자르다[잘라 내다]   (작은 나뭇가지 자르는) 낫
at last, with great difficulty, brought down the
마침내, 결국   어려움, 곤란, 역경
tree.

He began to fell another and the same thing
또 다른   같은
was repeated. He struggled and struggled and
반복하다, 되풀이하다   고군분투하다, 힘겹게 ~하다
succeeded only after great exertion.
성공하다, 해내다   노력, 분투

151

He began on a third and the same thing happened. Ivan had intended to fell fifty trees at
의도[작정]하다, (…하려고) 생각하다
least, and he had not managed more than ten,
~이상의
and night was coming on.

Ivan was exhausted, and the steam rose
기진맥진하다, 완전히 지치다 · 김, 증기
from him and floated through the wood like a
떠[흘러]가다[떠돌다]
mist; yet still he would not give up. He felled an-
엷은 안개, 박무 · 포기하다
other tree and his back began to ache so that he
아픈
could not go on. He stuck his axe into the trunk
도끼 · 나무 몸통
of a tree and sat down to rest.
쉬다, 휴식하다
When the Devilkin realized that Ivan had
깨닫다, 알아차리다
ceased to work, he rejoiced.
중단되다, 그치다 · 크게[대단히] 기뻐하다
"He is worn out at last," he thought; "now I
몹시 고단하다[지치다/피곤하다]
can rest too."

And he sat himself astride on a branch,
두 다리[발]를 쫙 벌리고
exulting.
환희하는, 기뻐 날뛰는, 의기양양한
Ivan rose, took out his axe, flourished it
휘두르다
aloft, and brought it down so heavily that the
하늘[위로] 높이 · 세게, 힘껏
tree came down with a crash. The Devilkin had
요란한 소리, 굉음
no time to disentangle his legs; the branch broke
엉킴을 풀다 · 나뭇가지
and pinned down his paw.
(동물의 발톱이 달린) 발

152

Ivan began to clear the tree and behold!
there was a live Devilkin. Ivan was amazed.

"You horrid little wretch! You here again!"

"I am not the same one," the Devilkin said. "I
belong to your brother Taras."

"Whoever you may be, you shall share the
same fate."

And Ivan raised the axe to bring it down on
its head, but the Devilkin began to plead.

"Don't kill me," he said, "and I'll do whatever
you want me to."

"What can you do?"

"I can make as much money as you like."

"Very well," Ivan said; "make it, then."

And the Devilkin taught him what to do.

"Take some leaves from this oak and rub
them in your hands and gold will fall to the
ground."

Ivan took the leaves and rubbed them in his
hand and gold rained down.

"This is well," he said; "on holidays it will amuse the children."

"Let me go," the Devilkin begged.

"I don't mind," Ivan said, and taking up his axe, he freed the Devilkin of the branch. "Go, in God's name."

At the mention of God the Devilkin plunged into the ground like a stone thrown into water, and there was nothing but the hole left.

6

The brothers built themselves houses and
began to live apart. Ivan finished his work
in the fields, brewed some beer and invited his
brothers to a feast. The brothers did not accept
his invitation.

"We do not go to feast with peasants," they
said.

Ivan treated the peasants and the peasant-
women and drank himself until he got tipsy,
and he went into the street and joined the danc-
ers and singers. He approached the women, and
bade them sing his praises.

"I will give you something you have never seen in your lives," he said.

The women laughed and began to sing his praises, and when they had finished, they said, "Well, give us what you promised."

"I will bring it in a moment," Ivan said, and he took his seed-basket and ran into the wood.

The women laughed.

"What a fool!" they said, and forgot all about him, when behold! Ivan returned, his basket full of something.

"Shall I share it out?"

"Do."

Ivan took up a handful of gold and threw it to the women. Heavens! The women rushed to pick it up, the peasants after them, snatching it out of each others' hands. One old woman was nearly killed in the fray.

Ivan laughed.

"You fools!" he said. "Why did you hurt Granny? If you are not so rough I'll give you some more."

He scattered more gold. The whole village
came up. Ivan emptied his basket. The people
asked for more, but he said, "Not now; another
time I'll give you more. Now let us dance. You
play some songs."

The women began to play.

"I don't like your songs," Ivan said.

"Do you know any better ones?"

"You shall see in a moment."

Ivan went into a barn, took up a sheaf,
thrashed it, stood it up, and banged it on the
floor, and said—

My slave bids you be a sheaf no more.
Every straw contained in you
Must turn into a soldier true.

And the sheaf burst asunder and turned into
soldiers, and the drummers and buglers played
at their head. Ivan asked the soldiers to play

157

some songs, and led them into the street.

이끌다

The people were amazed.

깜짝 놀라다

When the soldiers had played their songs

Ivan took them back into the barn, forbidding

헛간, 곳간 금지하다, 못하게 하다

any one to follow.

뒤따르다

He turned the soldiers into a sheaf again and

threw it on a pile of straw, then he went home

던지다   더미

and lay down to sleep in the stables.

마구간

7

Simon the Warrior heard of these things next morning, and went to his brother.

"Tell me," he said, "where did you get the soldiers from, and where did you take them to?"

"What does it matter to you?"

"Matter, indeed! With soldiers one can do anything. One can conquer a kingdom."

Ivan wondered.

"Really! Then why didn't you tell me before?" he said. "I will make you as many soldiers as you like. It is well Malania and I have threshed so much straw."

Ivan took his brother to the barn and said, "Look here, if I make the soldiers you must take them away at once, for if we have to feed them they will eat up the whole village in a day."

Simon the Warrior promised to take the soldiers away, and Ivan began to make them.

He banged a sheaf on the threshing-floor and a company appeared.

He banged another sheaf and a second company appeared. He made so many soldiers that they filled the whole field.

"Are there enough now?" he asked.

Simon was overjoyed and said, "That will do, Ivan, thank you."

"Very well. If you want more, come back and I'll make them for you. There is plenty of straw this year."

Simon the Warrior soon put his troops in order, and went away to make war.

He had no sooner gone than Taras the Pot-bellied came along. He, too, had heard of yester-

day's affair and he said to his brother, "Tell me
where you get gold money from. If only I could
get hold of some I could make it bring in money
from the whole world."

Ivan wondered.

"Really? Then why didn't you tell me before?
I'll make you as much as you like."

Taras was overjoyed.

"I shall be satisfied with three baskets full,"
he said.

"Very well; come into the wood," Ivan said;
"but I had better harness the mare, for you
won't be able to carry it away."

They rode into the wood. Ivan began to rub
the oak leaves, and made a heap of gold.

"Is it enough?" he asked.

Taras was overjoyed.

"It will do for the present, thank you, Ivan,"
he said.

"Very well," Ivan said; "if you want more,
come back and I'll make it for you. There are

plenty of leaves left."
많은

Taras the Pot-bellied gathered up a whole
모으다
cartload of money, and went off to trade.
수레[마차] 한 대분의 짐   떠나다   거래[교역/무역]하다

Both brothers had gone—Simon to make
war and Taras to trade. And Simon the Warrior
conquered a kingdom, and Taras the Pot-bellied
정복하다   왕국
made much money in trade.
돈을 많이 벌다

When the two brothers met they told each
만나다(meet)
other how they had come by their soldiers and
어떻게
money.

Simon the Warrior said to his brother, "I
have conquered a kingdom for myself and live
정복하다
well, only I have not enough money to feed my
충분한   먹이다
soldiers."

And Taras the Pot-bellied said, "I have made
a heap of money, only unfortunately I have no
더미, 무더기   불행하게도, 유감스럽게도
one to guard it."
지키다, 보호하다, 경비를 보다

And Simon the Warrior said, "Let us go to
our brother Ivan. I will ask him to make more
청하다, 부탁하다
soldiers and give them to you to guard your
지키다, 경비하다
money, and you must ask him to make more

money and give it to me to feed my soldiers."

And they came to Ivan.

And Simon said, "I haven't enough soldiers, brother. Will you make another couple of sheaves for me?"

Ivan shook his head.

"No," he said; "I won't make you any more soldiers."

"But you promised you would."

"I know I promised, but I won't make any more."

"Why not, you fool?"

"Because your soldiers killed a man. I will not let you have any more."

And he was obstinate, and would not make any more soldiers.

Then Taras the Pot-bellied asked Ivan the Fool to make him more golden money.

Ivan shook his head.

"No," he said; "I won't make any more money."

"But you promised."

"I know I promised, but I won't make any more."

"Why not, you fool?"

"Because your money took a cow away from a woman in the village."

"But how can that be?"

"The woman had a cow. The children used to drink the milk, but the other day they came to beg a little milk of me.

'But where's your cow?' I asked them, and they said, 'Taras' bailiff came and gave mother three golden coins and she gave him the cow; now we have no milk to drink.'

I thought you only wanted to play with the golden coins, but you've taken away the cow from the children; I won't give you any more."

And the Fool was obstinate and kept to his word.

And the brothers went away and deliberated
over their difficult situation in order to find a
way out.

Simon said, "This is what we must do. You
give me some of your money to feed my soldiers,
and I'll give you half my kingdom and soldiers
to guard your money."

Taras agreed. The brothers divided their
possessions, and both became kings and both
were rich.

8

And Ivan lived at home, supporting his father and mother and working in the fields
지원하다, 부양하다
일하다   들판
with his deaf and dumb sister.
농아

One day Ivan's yard-dog fell sick. He grew
집 마당에서 키우는 개   아픈, 병든
mangy, and was near dying. Ivan pitied it. He
(기생충으로 인한) 피부병에 걸린   불쌍히 여기다, 동정하다
took a piece of bread from his sister, put it in his
빵 한 조각
cap, carried it out and threw it to the dog.
모자   던지다

The creases in his cap parted and out rolled
주름, 구김살   구르다
one of the little roots with the bread. The dog
뿌리
ate it up. As soon as it had swallowed the root it
~하자마자   삼키다
began to jump about and bark and play and wag
짖다   흔들다
its tail. It was quite well again.
건강한

The father and mother were amazed.
깜짝 놀라게 하다

"How did you cure the dog?" they asked.

And Ivan said, "I had two little roots that could cure any pain, and the dog swallowed one."

It happened at the time that the King's daughter fell ill, and the King proclaimed to every town and village that he would reward any man who could cure her, and that if he were an unmarried man he should have her for his wife. The news came to Ivan's village.

And the father and mother summoned Ivan and said to him, "Have you heard of the King's promise? You told us you had a little root that could cure any sickness; go, cure the King's daughter, you will then be happy for life."

"Very well," Ivan said, "I will go."

And Ivan prepared himself for the journey, and they dressed him in his best clothes. When he came out on the doorstep he saw a beggar-woman with a crippled hand.

"I heard that you can cure the sick," she said. "Cure my hand, for I cannot even put on my

~도, ~조차

own shoes."

"Very well," Ivan said. And he took the little root out of his cap, gave it to the beggar-woman

거지 여인

and told her to swallow it. As soon as she swal-

삼키다   ~하자마자

lowed it, she recovered, and began to wave her

(정상 상태로) 회복되다   흔들다

hand.

The father and mother came out to bid good-

(인사를) 하다

bye to Ivan, and they heard that he had given away his last root and had nothing left with

마지막   남다

which to cure the King's daughter, and they be-

gan to scold him.

꾸짖다

"You pity a beggar-woman, yet have no pity

동정하다, 불쌍히 여기다

for the King's daughter," they reproached him.

(실망하여) 비난[책망]하다

But Ivan was sorry for the King's daughter.

He harnessed the mare, threw some straw into

마구를 채우다   암말, 암소   던지다(throw)

the cart and got in.

"Where are you going to, you fool?"

"To cure the King's daughter."

"But you have nothing to cure her with now."

168

"It doesn't matter," he said, and drove away.

He came to the King's palace, and as soon as he stepped over the threshold the King's daughter got well.

The King was overjoyed. He ordered Ivan to be brought to him, and dressed him in fine clothes.

"You must be my son-in-law," he said.

"Very well," Ivan said.

And Ivan married the princess. Her father died soon after, and Ivan became King.

All three brothers were now kings.

9

The three brothers lived and reigned.
The elder brother Simon the Warrior
lived well. With his straw soldiers he gathered
together real soldiers.

Throughout the whole of his kingdom he
ordered a levy of one soldier for every ten houses, and each soldier had to be tall and whole of
body and clean of face.

In this way he gathered many soldiers and
trained them. If any one opposed him he sent
his soldiers off at once and imposed his will, and
people began to fear him. His life was a very
goodly one.

Whatever he saw and wanted was his. He sent his soldiers and they brought him all he wanted.

Taras the Pot-bellied also lived well. He did not lose the money Ivan had given him, but increased it a hundredfold. He introduced law and order into his kingdom.

He stowed his money away in coffers and levied taxes on the people. There was a poll-tax, and tolls for walking and driving, and a tax on shoes and stockings and frills.

He got whatever he wanted. For money people brought him everything, and even worked for him, for every one wanted money.

Ivan the Fool, too, did not live badly. As soon as his father-in-law was dead, he took off his royal robes and gave them to his wife to stow away in a chest.

And he put on his coarse linen shirt and breeches and peasant shoes and began to work once more.

"It's so dull for me," he said. "I've got fat, lost
my appetite and can't sleep."

He brought his father and mother and sister
to live with him, and began to work as of old.

"But you are a king," people remonstrated.

"Even a king must eat," he said.

One of his ministers came to him and said,
"We have no money to pay salaries."

"Don't pay them, then," he said.

"But no one will serve us."

"What does it matter? They needn't. They'll
have more time for work. There's the manure to
cart; heaps of it lying about."

When people came to Ivan for justice and
said, "That man stole my money."

Ivan said, "Never mind; he must have wanted it."

And all realized that Ivan was a fool.

And his wife said to him, "People say you are
a fool."

"What does it matter?" Ivan said.

His wife reflected awhile, but she was also a fool.

"Why should I go against my husband?" she said. "Where the needle goes, the thread follows."

So she took off her royal robes, put them away in a chest and went to Malania to learn to work. When she knew how, she began to help her husband.

All the wise left Ivan's kingdom, and only the fools remained.

Nobody had money. They lived and worked, fed themselves and others.

10

The old Devil waited and waited for news of the Devilkins. He was expecting to hear that they had ruined the three brothers, but no news came. He set out himself to find them. He searched and searched, and found nothing but three holes.

"They've not been able to manage it, evidently," he thought. "I must tackle the job myself."

He went to look for the brothers, but they were no longer in their old places. He found them in their different kingdoms. All three lived and reigned. The old Devil was annoyed.

"Now we'll see what I can do!" he said.

First of all he went to King Simon.
가장 먼저, 무엇보다 먼저

He did not go in his own shape, but dis-
모양, 형태　변장하다

guised himself as a general. In that guise he ap-
장군　(가장된) 겉모습[외피]

peared before King Simon.

"I have heard that you are a great warrior,
위대한, 커다란

King Simon," he said. "I am well versed in these
(~에) 정통한[조예가 깊은]

things and want to serve you."
섬기다, 봉사하다

And King Simon began to ask him all man-
시작하다　묻다　온갖 종류의 ~

ner of questions, and seeing that he was a clever
질문　영리한, 똑똑한

man, he took him into his service.
서비스, 봉사

The new commander instructed King Simon
지휘관, 사령관　(기술을) 가르치다, (정보를) 알려 주다

how to collect a large army.
모으다, 수집하다

"First of all," he said, "we must get more
얻다, 갖다

soldiers. There are many idle people in your
군인　게으른, 가동되지 않는, 놀고 있는

kingdom. We must conscript all the young men
징집[징병]하다

without exception, then you will have an army
예외　군대, 부대

five times as large as the one you have now.
5배

"Secondly, we must get new guns and can-
둘째, 두 번째　총　대포

nons. I will get guns that will fire a hundred

bullets at one shot; they will rain out like peas.
총알　(총기) 발사, 발포　완두콩

And I will get cannons that will consume with
전소시키다, 휩싸다

175

fire either man or horse or wall; they will burn
말   벽   불태우다
everything."

King Simon listened to the new comman-
경청하다, 귀 기울여 듣다   지휘관, 사령관
der, and enrolled all the young men as soldiers
병적에 넣다(enlist), 등록하다
and built new factories where he manufactured
짓다, 건설하다   공장   (대량으로) 제조[생산]하다
new guns and cannons, then he made war on a
총   대포   전쟁
neighbouring king.
이웃의, 이웃해 있는
As soon as he was faced by the opposing
~하자마자   대하다, 마주하다   서로 싸우는 (상대방의)
army, King Simon ordered his soldiers to rain
명령하다, 지시하다
bullets against it and shoot fire from their can-
총알
nons, in this way wiping out half the hostile
~을 완전히 파괴하다[없애 버리다]   적대적인
troops. The neighbouring king was alarmed; he
군대, 부대   깜짝 놀라게 하다
surrendered and gave up his kingdom. King Si-
항복[굴복]하다(=give in)
mon rejoiced.
크게[대단히] 기뻐하다
"Now," he said, "I will make war on the King

of India."

And the King of India heard of King Simon's

doings. He adopted all his methods, and in-
쓰다, 취하다, 채택하다   방법, 체계, 수단, 수법
vented some improvements of his own. He not
향상, 개선, 호전
only enrolled all the young men as soldiers, but
등록하다
the unmarried women as well, and in conse-
결혼하지 않은   여자   그 결과(로서)

quence had a larger army than King Simon. And
he made guns and cannons like King Simon's,
and invented machines to fly in the air and drop
발명하다   기계   날다   떨어뜨리다
explosive bombs from above.
폭발성의, 폭발하기 쉬운 폭탄

And King Simon set out to make war on the
출발하다, 시작하다, 착수하다
King of India, thinking he would beat him as
때리다, 이기다
easily as he had beaten the other king, but the
쉽게
scythe that had cut so well had lost its edge.
큰 낫   (칼 등의) 날

The King of India did not give Simon time to
open fire, for he sent his women to fly in the air
보내다
and drop explosive bombs on Simon's troops.
폭발성의, 잘 터지는 폭탄   부대, 군대
And the women rained down bombs from above
like borax upon cockroaches and Simon's troops
붕사(분산 나트륨의 결정체) 바퀴벌레
scattered and fled, and Simon was left alone.
(사방으로) 흩어지다 달아나다(flee)

The King of India took possession of Simon's
재산, 소지품
kingdom, and Simon the Warrior escaped as
도망치다, 달아나다
best he could.

Having disposed of this brother, the old
~을 없애다[처리하다]
Devil went to King Taras.

He changed himself into a merchant and
바꾸다, 변하다   상인
settled in Taras' kingdom, where he opened

establishments and began to circulate money
창립, 설립, 기관, 시설   순환하다, 순환시키다

freely. He paid high prices for everything, and
값, 가격

the people flocked to him for the sake of the ex-
(많은 수가) 모이다, 떼 지어 가다[오다]

tra profit.
이익, 수익, 이윤

And the people came to have so much mon-

ey that they were able to settle all their arrears
해결하다, 정리하다   지불 잔금, 연체금

and to pay their taxes at the proper time. King
적절한, 제대로 된

Taras rejoiced.

"Thanks to the merchant," he thought, "I
감사하다   상인   생각하다

have more money than ever, and I'll be able to
더 많은, 더욱

live better than I used to."

And he began making all sorts of new plans,
종류, 부류   계획, 플랜

and decided to have a new palace built for him-
결정하다   궁전, 왕궁

self.

He proclaimed to the people that he wanted
선언[선포]하다(=declare)

timber and stone and labour, for which he was
목재, 재목   돌멩이   (육체적인) 노동[작업]

prepared to pay a high price. King Taras thought
준비하다   지불하다   값, 가격

that for his money people would flock to work
떼 지어 가다[오다/ 모이다]

for him as of old. But lo! all the timber and stone
야, 하!(감탄사)

was taken to the merchant, and all the labourers

flocked to work for him. King

Taras raised his price, and the merchant raised his. King Taras had much money, but the merchant had more and beat the King. The King's palace could not be built.

King Taras had arranged to make a new garden. When the autumn came he proclaimed that he wanted men to come and plant his garden, but no one came, for the people were all digging for the merchant.

Winter came. King Taras wanted to buy some sable skins for a new coat. He sent a messenger to buy it, but the messenger returned empty-handed, and said that there were no sable skins, for the merchant had bought them all at a higher price, and made himself a sable carpet.

King Taras wanted to buy some stallions. He sent a messenger, but the messenger returned and said that the merchant had all the good stallions; they were carting water for him to make a pond.

And the King's plans fell to pieces, for no
계획, 플랜 너덜너덜해지다(=fall apart)
one would work for him. All worked for the
merchant, and only brought him the merchant's
오직, 단지
money to pay the taxes.
지불하다   세금

And the King came to have so much money
that he did not know where to put it all, but he
lived badly. The King gave up making plans;
나쁘게, 불쾌하게   포기하다   계획
he would have been contented to live quietly
~에 자족하다   조용히
somehow, but even that was difficult. He was
어떻게든   어려운, 곤란한
hampered on all sides. His cook and coachman
방해하다(=hinder)   요리사   마부
and servants left him to go to the merchant's.
하인   떠나다

He even went short of food. When he sent to
부족, 결핍
the market to buy some provisions there were
시장   식량, 양식
none left, for the merchant had bought up everything, and the people only brought the King
money for their taxes.

King Taras lost patience and banished the
인내심   (국외로) 추방하다
merchant from his kingdom. The merchant
settled on the very border, and did exactly the
정착하다   바로 국경   정확히
same as before, and for his money the people
dragged everything away from the King and

brought it to the merchant.

Life became very hard for the King. For whole days he did not eat, and to make matters worse a rumour went abroad that the merchant had boasted that he would buy the King himself. King Taras lost courage, and did not know what to do.

Simon the Warrior came to him and said, "Will you support me? I have been beaten by the King of India."

King Taras himself was in a sad plight.

"I haven't eaten anything myself for two days," he said.

11

Having disposed of the two brothers, the old Devil went to Ivan. He changed himself into a general and came to Ivan, and began to persuade him to set up a large army.

"A king should not live without an army," he said. "Give me the power, and I'll collect soldiers from among your people and organize an army."

Ivan listened to all he had to say.

"Very well," he said, "organize one, then; only teach the soldiers to sing nice songs, for I like singing."

And the old Devil went through Ivan's kingdom to collect a voluntary army. To each recruit who should offer himself he promised a bottle of vodka and a red cap.

The fools laughed at him.

"We have plenty of drink," they said; "we brew it ourselves, and as for caps, our women can make us any kind we like—embroidered ones and even ones with fringes."

And no one offered himself.

The old Devil went back to Ivan and said, "Your fools won't enlist of their own accord; we'll have to force them."

"Very well; force them, then."

And the old Devil proclaimed throughout the kingdom that every man must enlist as a soldier, and if he fails to do so Ivan will have him put to death.

The fools came to the Devil and said, "You tell us that if we won't enlist as soldiers the King will have us put to death, but you don't say what will happen to us when we become soldiers. People say that soldiers are killed."

"You can't get over that."

When the fools heard this they kept to their decision.

"We won't go," they said. "We'd sooner die at home since we have to die in either case."

"What fools you are!" the old Devil said. "A soldier may or may not be killed, but if you don't go King Ivan will have you put to death for certain."

The fools reflected over this; then went to Ivan the Fool and said, "A general has appeared among us who orders us all to enlist as soldiers. 'If you go as a soldier,' he says, 'you may or you may not be killed, but if you don't go, King Ivan will have you put to death for certain.' Is it true?"

Ivan laughed.

"How can I alone have you all put to death? Had I not been a fool I would have explained it to you, but I don't understand it myself."

"Then we won't go," the fools said.

"Very well, don't."

The fools went to the general and refused to enlist as soldiers.

The old Devil saw that his plan would not work, so he went to the King of Tarakan and wormed himself into his favour.

"Come," he said, "let us go and make war on King Ivan. He has no money, but grain and cattle and all manner of good things he has in abundance."

The King of Tarakan prepared to make war. He gathered together a large army, repaired his guns and cannons and marched across the border on his way to Ivan's kingdom.

People came to Ivan and said, "The King of Tarakan is marching on us with his army."

"Very well; let him," Ivan said.

When the King of Tarakan crossed the border he sent his vanguard to find Ivan's troops. They searched and searched, but no troops were to be found anywhere.

Should they wait and see if they showed
기다리다 보여주다
themselves? But there was no sign of any troops
신호, 징후
and no one to fight with.
싸우다

The King of Tarakan sent men to seize the
보내다 장악하다, 점령하다
villages. The soldiers came to one village and the
마을
fools—men and women alike—rushed out and
바보 달려나오다
stood gaping at them in wonder.
(놀라서) 입을 딱 벌리고 바라보다

The soldiers began to take away their corn
빼앗다, 가져가다 곡식
and cattle and the fools let them have what they
소 내버려 두다
wanted, making no resistance.
저항, 항거

The soldiers went to another village and the
또 다른
same thing was repeated. And they marched
되풀이하다, 반복하다
one day and another, and still the same thing
happened.

Everything was given up without any resis-
포기하다
tance and the fools even invited the soldiers to
초대하다
stay with them.

"If you find it hard to live in your parts, good

fellows, come and settle with us altogether."
정착하다
And the soldiers marched from village to vil-

lage and no troops were to be found anywhere;

the people lived, fed themselves and others; no
먹이다, 먹여 살리다
one offered any resistance and every one invited
주다, 제공하다   저항, 항거, 반대   초대하다
them to settle there.

And the soldiers grew weary of the job and
···에 진절머리가 나다.
they went back to their King of Tarakan.

"We can't fight here," they said; "take us to
싸우다
another place. This is not war; this is child's-
전쟁, 전투
play. We can't fight here."

The King of Tarakan grew angry. He ordered
화난, 성난   명령하다
his soldiers to go over the whole kingdom and
전체의, 전부의
lay waste the villages and burn the corn and kill
~을 초토화하다   불태우다
the cattle.

"If you won't do what I tell you," he said, "I
will punish you all."
처벌하다, 벌주다
The soldiers were frightened and began to
겁먹게[놀라게] 만들다
carry out the King's commands. They burnt the
수행하다, 행동에 옮기다   명령, 지시
houses and corn and killed the cattle.

The fools made no resistance, they only
wept. The old men wept and the old women and
울다, 눈물을 흘리다(weep)
the little children.

"Why do you treat us like this?" they said.
대하다, 대접하다

"Why do you waste the good things? If you want
낭비하다, 못 쓰게 만들다

them, why not take them?"

And the soldiers grew to loathe their work.
혐오하다(=detest)

They refused to go further and the troops
거절하다, 거부하다   더 멀리에   군대, 부대

dispersed.
(이리저리) 흩어지다, 해산하다

12

And the old Devil went away, having failed to bring Ivan to reason by means of the soldiers.

The old Devil changed himself into a clean gentleman and came to live in Ivan's kingdom, hoping to ruin Ivan by money, as he had done Taras.

"I want to do you good and teach you common sense," he said. "I will build myself a house in your midst and open an establishment."

"Very well," the people said; "you can live here."

The clean gentleman spent the night and in the morning he went out to the square with a bag of gold and a bundle of papers and said, "You all live like swine. I want to teach you how you ought to live. Build me a house according to this plan. You will work for me and I will teach you and pay you in golden money."

And he showed them the gold.

The fools marvelled. They had no money in circulation, but exchanged thing for thing, or paid by labour. And they began to exchange things with the gentleman and to work for his golden coins.

And the old Devil, as in Taras' kingdom, began to circulate gold, and people brought him things and worked for him.

The old Devil rejoiced.

"At last my plan is beginning to work!" he thought. "I will ruin him as I ruined Taras, and will get him completely in my power."

The fools collected the golden coins and gave

them to the women to make themselves neck-
laces and to the girls to plait into their hair; the
children even played with the coins in the street.
After a while every one had enough and refused to take more. And the clean gentleman's
house was not half finished, and the corn and
cattle had not yet been stored up for the year.

And the gentleman invited people to come
and work for him to bring him corn and rear his
cattle, offering to pay many golden coins for everything brought and every piece of work done.

But no one would come and work, and no
one would bring him anything, unless a chance
boy or girl brought him an egg in exchange for
a golden coin; and no one else came and he was
left without any food.

And the clean gentleman was hungry and
went through the village to buy himself something for dinner. He went into one house and
offered a golden coin for a chicken, but the mistress would not take it.

"I have many such coins," she said.

He went into another place to buy a salt her-
곳, 장소　　　　　　　염장한 청어
ring, offering a golden piece.

"I don't want it, my good man," the mistress
여주인
said. "I have no children to play with them, and
have three of these pieces already as curiosities."
이미, 벌써　　　호기심
He went into a peasant's for some bread.
농부　　　　　　빵
The peasant too would not take the money.

"I don't want it," he said. "But if you want
the bread in Christ's name, then wait, and I'll
그리스도　　　　　　　　기다리다
tell my old woman to cut you some."

The old Devil spat on the ground and fled
침을 뱉다　　　땅바닥　　　　도망치다
from the peasant. To hear the word Christ was
듣다　　　단어
worse than a knife to him, let alone to take any-
~보다 더 나쁜　　　　　　　~커녕, ~은 고사하고
thing in His name.

And so he got no bread. All had gold; wher-
얻다, 갖다
ever the old Devil went no one would give him
악마　　　　　　　　　주다
anything for money, and every one said, "Bring
돈을 바라고, 돈으로
us something else instead, or come and work, or
(또) 다른 것　　　　대신에
take it in Christ's name."

And the Devil had nothing to offer but money and had no liking for work, and he could not take anything in Christ's name.

He lost his temper.

"What more do you want when I offer you money?" he said. "You can buy anything you like for gold and employ any kind of labour."

But the fools did not heed him.

"We don't need money," they said. "We exchange everything in kind and have no taxes to pay; what good would it be to us?"

The old Devil went supperless to bed.

The story reached Ivan the Fool. People came to him and said, "What shall we do? A clean gentleman has appeared in our midst who likes to eat and drink well, and dress in fine clothes, but he won't work and won't take anything in Christ's name; he only offers us golden coins. People gave him what he wanted until they had enough of these coins, and now no one gives him anything. What are we to do with him? He may die of hunger."

Ivan listened to what they had to say.

"He must be fed, certainly. Let him act as a shepherd to you all in turn."

Since there was no way out, the old Devil had to go about shepherding. He went from house to house until it came to Ivan's turn.

The old Devil came in to dinner and the deaf and dumb girl was getting it ready. She had often been deceived by lazy folk who came in early to dinner without having done their share of work and ate up all the porridge, so she invented a means of finding out the sluggards by their hands. Those who had horny hands were put at the table; the others were given the leavings.

The old Devil sat down by the table, but the deaf and dumb girl seized him by the hands and looked at them to see if they had any blisters, but they were clean and smooth and the finger nails were long. The girl grunted and pulled the old Devil away from the table.

Ivan's wife said to him, "Don't be offended,

fine gentleman. My sister-in-law never lets any one sit at the table who hasn't horny hands. In good time, when the others have finished, you shall get what is left."

And the old Devil was hurt that in the King's house they should want to feed him with the pigs.

And he said to Ivan, "What a stupid custom there is in your kingdom that all people must work with their hands! I suppose you were too stupid to think of anything else. Do you think it's only with the hands people work? Do you know what wise men work with?"

And Ivan said, "How are we fools to know; we work only with our hands and backs."

"That is because you are fools. I will teach you how to work with the head, then you will know that it is more profitable than to work with the hands."

Ivan wondered.

"Really! No wonder people call us fools!"

And the old Devil said, "Only it's not easy to work with the head. You won't give me any dinner because my hands are smooth, but you don't know that it's a hundred times harder to work with the head. Sometimes one's head nearly splits."

Ivan grew thoughtful.

"Why should you torture yourself so, my good man? Wouldn't it be better to do the easier work with your hands and back?"

And the Devil said, "I torture myself because I pity you fools. If I were not to torture myself you would remain fools for ever. I have worked with the head and now I'm going to teach you."

Ivan wondered.

"Teach us, then," he said, "so that when our hands are tired we can work with the head."

The Devil promised to teach them.

And Ivan proclaimed throughout his kingdom that a clean gentleman had appeared among them who would teach every one to work with his head and that it was more profitable to work with the head than with the hands, and he bade every man come and hear him.

There was a high tower in Ivan's kingdom and a steep staircase leading up to it and there was a turret on the top.

And Ivan took the gentleman up the tower, so that he might be seen by all.

And the gentleman took his place on the top of the tower and began to speak, and the fools flocked to look at him.

They thought that the gentleman would really show them how to work with the head instead of the hands, but he merely told them in words how they could live without working at all. The fools did not understand him. They stared and stared, then went home to attend to their own affairs.

The old Devil stood on top of the tower one day and another, speaking all the time. He was hungry, but it never occurred to the fools to bring him some bread up the tower.

They thought that if he could work with the head better than with the hands, he could easily make himself some bread.

The old Devil stood on the tower for another day, still speaking. The people came and stared at him for a while; then went their ways.

"Well, has the gentleman begun to work with his head?" Ivan asked.

"Not yet; he is still jabbering."

The Devil stood on the tower for another day and began to grow faint. He swayed and knocked his head against a pillar.

One of the fools saw him and told Ivan's wife, who hastened to Ivan at the ploughing.

"Come, come," she said. "They say the gentleman has begun to work with his head."

Ivan wondered.

"Really?" he said, and turning his horse round, he went to the tower.

When he got there, the old Devil, who was
이르다, 도착하다
quite faint with hunger by this time, was stag-
꽤, 상당히   비틀[휘청]거리다
gering and knocking his head against the pillars,
· 두드리다
and when Ivan came up, he fell with a crash
떨어지다   요란한 소리를 내며
down the stairs, counting each step on the way
계단   (수를) 세다   각각의
with a knock of his head.

"Well," Ivan said, "the clean gentleman
spoke truly when he said that the head splits
진실로, 진짜로   쪼개지다
sometimes. Blisters on the hands are nothing to
물집, 수포
this; after such work there will be bumps on the
(~에) 부딪치다
head."

The old Devil fell to the bottom of the stairs
밑바닥
and thumped his head against the ground.
쿵[탁] 하고 떨어지다
Ivan was about to go up and see how much
막 ~하려고 하다
work he had done, when suddenly the earth
갑자기, 별안간   땅
opened and the old Devil fell through. Only a
hole was left.
구멍   남다
Ivan scratched his head.
긁다
"You horrid wretch! One of those devils
진저리나는   악마 같은[비열한] 인간   악마
again! The father of the others, no doubt. What
나머지, 다른 사람들 분명히, 틀림없이
a huge one too!"
거대한, 엄청나게 큰

Ivan is living to this day and people flock to
his kingdom.

His own brothers have come to him and he
supports them. When any one comes and says,
"Feed me," Ivan says, "Very well, you can live
with us; we have plenty of everything."

Only there is a special custom in his kingdom—whoever has horny hands comes to table;
whoever has smooth ones eats the leavings.

에멜리안과 빈 북

EMELIAN AND
THE EMPTY DRUM

Emelian was a labourer and worked for a
master. He was walking through a field
one day on his way to work, when a frog hopped
in front of him and he just missed crushing it by
stepping across.

Suddenly some one called to him from
behind. He turned, and there stood a beauti-
ful maiden, who said to him, "Why don't you
marry, Emelian?"

"How can I, dear maiden? I possess nothing
but the clothes I stand up in, and who would
have a husband like that?"

"Marry me," the maiden said.

Emelian looked at her in admiration.
감탄, 존경

"I would with pleasure," he said, "but how
기쁨, 즐거움
should we live?"

"What a thing to trouble about, indeed!" the
것, 물건, 사물   괴롭히다, 애 먹이다   정말로, 실제로
maiden said. "One has only to work the more
일하다   더, 더욱
and sleep the less and one can always be clothed
더 적게 자다   늘, 항상   입다
and fed."
먹이다

"Very well; let us marry, then," Emelian said.
~하자   결혼하다
"Where shall we live?"
어디서

"In the town."
(소)도시, 읍
Emelian and the maiden went to the town.

She took him to a little house on the very edge
데리고 가다   작은   끝, ~가
and they married and set up housekeeping.
가정을 갖다, 살림을 꾸리다

One day the King went for a drive beyond
…저편에[너머]
the town, and when passing Emelian's gate,
지나가다   대문
Emelian's wife came out to look at him. When
아내   밖으로 나오다
the King saw her he marvelled.
감탄하다, 경탄하다

"What a beauty!" he thought. He stopped the
미인
carriage and called her to him.
마차   부르다

"Who are you?" he asked.
묻다

"Emelian the peasant's wife."
농부

"How came a beauty like you to marry a peasant?" he asked. "You should have been a queen."

"Thank you for your kind words," she said; "a peasant husband is good enough for me."

The King talked to her a while and went on his way. When he returned to the palace Emelian's wife did not go out of his head for a moment. The whole night he could not sleep and kept on thinking how he could take her away from Emelian, but no possible way occurred to him. He summoned his servants and asked them to think of a way.

And the servants said to him, "Get Emelian to come and be a labourer in the palace. We will wear him out with work, then his wife will become a widow and you can have her."

The King followed their advice. He sent a messenger to tell Emelian that he was to come and be a yard-porter in the palace and bring his wife to live with him there.

The messenger came to Emelian and repeated (반복하다, 되풀이하다) the King's words. And Emelian's wife said to her husband, "It can't be helped (어쩔 수 없다); you must go. You can work (일하다) there in the day and return to me at night (낮에는 ... 밤에는)."

Emelian went away. When he came to the palace (궁전) the King's steward (수위, 집사, 관리인) said to him, "Why have you come without (~없이) your wife?"

"Why should I drag (데려오다, 끌고 오다) her about with me? She has a home of her own (소유의)."

In the King's yard (뜰, 마당, 정원) Emelian was given enough work for two men. Emelian set about (~을 시작하다) it, not expecting (기대하다) to get it all finished (끝내다, 마치다), but behold (보라!) before evening (저녁) came it was all done (끝내다, 해내다).

The steward, seeing that he had got through ([일 따위]를 끝내다, 완수하다) the work, gave him four times as much (4배) for the morrow (내일).

Emelian went home. The house was scrubbed and cleaned (비눗물과 솔로) 문질러 씻다[청소하다], the fire lighted (불이 붙은[타고 있는]), the bread baked (~을 굽다), the supper (저녁식사) cooked (요리하다). His wife was sitting at the table sewing, waiting for him.

She flew to the door to meet him, then laid
the supper and fed him well; afterwards she began to ask him about his work.

"It's rather bad," he said; "they set me tasks
beyond my strength; they wear me out with too
much work."

"Don't you think about the work," she said,
"don't look back to see how much you have
done, nor look ahead to see how much there is
left. Just keep straight on and all will be done in
time."

Emelian went to bed. In the morning he
again set out to the palace. He began his work
and did not look round once, and behold! by
evening it was all finished; he went home when
it was still light.

Again they increased Emelian's work, but
Emelian finished it all in time and went home
for the night as usual.

A week passed. The King's servants saw that
they could not get the better of Emelian by giv-

ing him rough work so they gave him difficult
work instead, but even that did not help.

No matter what they set him to do—carpen-
tering, stone-cutting, thatching—he got everything done in time and went home for the night
to his wife. Another week passed.

The King summoned his servants and said,
"Is it for nothing that I keep you? Two weeks
have passed and still I do not see the fruits of
your work. You promised to wear Emelian out
with work and each night from my window I
see him going home singing to himself. Are you
making sport of me, eh?"

The King's servants began to excuse themselves.

"We are doing the best we can. We thought
at first to wear him out with rough work, but
you can't get him anyhow. We set him all kinds
of tasks, such as sweeping, but he doesn't know
what it means to be tired. Then we gave him
difficult work, thinking that he wouldn't have

brains enough to do it, yet still, we couldn't get
the better of him. No matter what the work, he
tackles it and gets it all done in time.

"He must either be extraordinarily strong
or his wife must be a witch. We are sick of him
ourselves. We want to set him such a task that
he cannot possibly do.

"We thought of asking him to build a temple
in a single day. You must send for him and command him to build a temple opposite the palace
in a single day, and if he fails to do it, we can cut
off his head for disobedience."

The King sent for Emelian.

"Build me a new temple in the square opposite the palace; by to-morrow evening it must all
be finished. If you do it, I will reward you; if not,
I will cut off your head."

Emelian listened to the King's words; then
turned and went his way home. When he got
there he said to his wife, "Make yourself ready,
wife; we must run away or else we are both lost."

208

"Why," she said, "have you grown so faint-hearted that you want to run away?"

"How can I help it when the King commanded me to build a temple to-morrow before nightfall? If I fail to do it, he will have my head cut off. There is only one way out. We must run away while there is yet time."

The wife did not approve of his words.

"The King has many soldiers; we shall not be able to escape them. And while you have strength enough you must obey the King's command."

"But how can I obey if it's beyond my strength?"

"My dear, don't get excited. Have your supper and go to bed; get up early in the morning and you'll manage in good time."

Emelian went to bed. His wife woke him in the morning.

"Go," she said; "make haste and finish the temple. Here are nails and a hammer. There is still a day's work for you left to do."

Emelian set out (출발하다). When he came to the square, there in the middle (~의 한가운데에) stood a new temple (광장 refers to square) not quite (꽤, 상당히) finished. Emelian set to work to finish it and by the evening it was all done.

The King awoke and looking out (내다보다) of the palace window (창문) he saw a new temple (성당, 신전) in the square (광장). Emelian was busy around (…하기에 바쁘다), knocking a nail (못) in here and there (여기저기에). The King was not pleased with (좋아하다, 달가워하다) the temple; he was annoyed (짜증나는, 성가신) that he had no pretext (구실, 핑계) for cutting off Emelian's head and taking (갖다, 취하다) his wife for himself.

Again (다시) the King summoned (부르다, 소환하다) his servants.

"Emelian has done this task (일, 과업, 과제) too," he said, "and I have no reason (이유, 근거) for cutting off his head. This was not difficult (어려운, 힘든, 까다로운) enough; we must give him something more difficult still. You decide (결정하다) what it shall be, or else (그렇지 않으면(=otherwise)) I'll have your heads cut off first."

And the servants bethought (잘 생각하다, 숙고하다(bethink)) them to set Emelian to make a river (강) that was to wind round

남다

210

the palace and have ships sailing on it.

The King summoned Emelian and set him the new task.

"If you could make a temple in a single night," he said, "you can do this too. See that it is all finished by to-morrow, or else I shall cut off your head."

Emelian's spirits fell lower than ever and he went home to his wife in a sad mood.

"Why so sad?" asked his wife. "Has the King set you a new task?"

Emelian told her what it was.

"We must run away," he concluded.

And the wife said, "We cannot escape the soldiers. You must obey."

"But how can I?"

"My dear, don't worry. Have your supper and go to bed. Get up early in the morning and all will be ready in time."

Emelian went to bed. In the morning his wife woke him.

"Go to the palace," she said; "everything is finished. Only by the harbour, opposite the palace, there is a little mound that wants levelling; take the spade and level it."

Emelian set out. He came to the town and there around the palace a river flowed with ships sailing on it. Emelian went up to the harbour opposite the palace and he saw an uneven place and began to level it.

The King awoke and looking out of his palace window he saw a river where there was not one before and ships were sailing on it and Emelian was levelling a little mound with his spade.

And the King was alarmed. He took no pleasure in the river or the ships, he was only annoyed that he could not cut off Emelian's head.

"There is no task he cannot do," he thought. "What shall we do now?"

And the King summoned his servants and conferred with them.

"Think of a task," he said, "that will be beyond Emelian's strength, for so far he has done everything we have thought of and I cannot take away his wife."

And the courtiers thought for a long time, then came to the King and said, "You must summon Emelian and say to him, 'Go to—I don't know where, and bring me—I don't know what.' He won't be able to escape you then, for wherever he goes you can say it was not the right place and whatever he brings was not the right thing. Then you can cut off his head and take away his wife."

The King was pleased with the idea. He sent for Emelian and said to him, "Go to—I don't know where, and bring me—I don't know what. And if you don't, I'll cut off your head."

Emelian went back to his wife and told her what the King had said. The wife reflected.

"Well," she said. "Be it on the King's own head what his courtiers have taught him. We must act with cunning now."

She sat and thought it over for a while; then said to her husband, "You must go a long way to our old grandmother, a peasant soldier's mother, and ask her to help you. She will give you something which you must take straight to the palace and I will be there already. I cannot escape them now; they will take me by force, but only for a short while. If you do what grandmother tells you, you will soon set me free."

And the wife prepared Emelian for the journey and gave him a bundle and a spindle.

"Give grandmother this spindle," she said; "by this she will know that you are my husband."

And the wife showed him the way. Emelian left the town and saw some soldiers drilling. He stopped and watched them.

The soldiers finished their drill and sat down to rest. Emelian approached them and asked, "Can you tell me, mates, how to get to—I don't know where and bring back—I don't know what."

The soldiers were perplexed at his words. "Who sent you?" they asked.

"The King," he said.

"We too," they said, "since the day we became soldiers want to go to—we don't know where and find—we don't know what, but we've never been able to find it and so cannot help you."

Emelian sat with the soldiers awhile then went on his way. He wandered and wandered till he came to a wood.

In the wood was a cottage and in the cottage sat an old woman, a peasant soldier's mother, spinning at her wheel, and she wept as she spun and moistened her fingers with the tears that flowed from her eyes.

"Who are you?" she cried in anger when she saw Emelian.

Emelian gave her the spindle and said that

his wife had sent him. The old woman instantly
즉시, 당장
softened and began to ask him questions.
부드러워지다   질문
And Emelian told her his whole story of how
전체의, 전부의
he had married the maiden and gone to live in
결혼하다   처녀
the town, and how he had been taken to the
소도시, 읍
King's as a yard-porter, and of the work he had
마당지기, 정원 일꾼
done in the palace, and the temple he had built
궁전   신전, 사원, 성당   짓다
in a night, and the river and ships he had made,
강   배
and that now the King had sent him to—I don't
know where to bring back—I don't know what.

The old woman listened to what he had to
경청하다, 귀 기울여 듣다
say and ceased her weeping. She began to mut-
멈추다, 중단하다   울음   중얼거리다
ter to herself, "The time has come, I see. Very
시간, 때
well," she said aloud; "sit down, my son, and
큰소리로, 크게
have something to eat."

Emelian had something to eat and the old
woman said to him, "Here is a ball of thread;
실꾸리, 실뭉치
roll it before you and follow wherever it leads.
굴리다   ~앞에   따라가다   어디든   이끌다
You will have to go a long way, to the very sea.

When you come to the sea you will see a large

town. Ask to be allowed to stay the night in the
허락하다, 용납하다

216

outermost house and look for what you want
가장 바깥쪽의   ~을 찾다
there."

"But by what signs shall I know it, grand-
                    신호, 조짐
mother?"

"When you see that which men listen to
                                        경청하다
more than to father or mother, that will be the
~보다 더
thing you want. Seize it and take it to the King.
물건, 사물   꽉 붙잡다
He will tell you you haven't brought the right
        말하다   가져오다
thing, and you must say to him, 'If it is not the
                    말하다
right thing then I must break it.' Then strike
                        깨다, 부수다   세게 치다
this thing; carry it out to the river; break it and
        나르다, 운반하다   강   부수다, 깨다
throw it into the water. Then you will get back
던지다   되찾다
your wife and dry up my tears."
                        마르다
Emelian took leave of the grandmother and
went where the ball of thread took him to. The
                    실뭉치
ball rolled and rolled till it brought him to the
구르다   ~까지
sea, where there was a large town.
                                큰, 커다란
Emelian knocked at a house and asked to be
두드리다, 노크하다   요청하다, 부탁하다
allowed to stay the night. The people let him in.
허락하다   묵다, 머물다
He went to bed.

In the morning he woke early and heard the

father of the house trying to wake his son to
chop some wood.

The son would not listen to him.

"It is early yet," he said, "there's plenty of
time."

And he heard the mother near the stove say,
"Do go, my son. Your father's bones ache; surely
you wouldn't let him go? Get up."

The son only smacked his lips and went
to sleep again. He had no sooner fallen asleep
than there was a banging and a rumbling in the
street. The son jumped up, dressed and ran out.
Emelian ran out after him to see what it was
that a son obeyed more than father or mother.
When Emelian got outside he saw a man
coming up the street carrying some round object
on his belly that he was beating with sticks. It
was this thing that had made the noise and that
the son had obeyed. Emelian approached and
examined it. The thing was round like a small
tub with skin drawn tightly on either side of it.

"What is this thing called?" he asked.
부르다

"A drum," they said.
북, 드럼

"Is it empty?"
속이 빈, 텅 빈

"Yes," they said.

Emelian wondered and asked the people to
놀라다, 감탄하다   요청하다, 부탁하다
give him the thing, but they would not.

Emelian gave up asking and followed the
포기하다   따라가다
drummer. He walked about the whole day and
북 치는 사람   걸어가다   온전한, 전부의
when the drummer went to bed at night, Eme-

lian seized the drum and ran away with it.
와락[꽉] 붙잡다   도망치다

He ran and ran until he came to his own

town. He wanted to give his wife a surprise, but
뜻밖의[놀라운] 일[소식]
she was not at home. She had been taken to the

King the day after Emelian had left.
다음 날   떠나다

Emelian went to the palace and asked to be

announced as the man who had gone to—I don't
발표하다, 알리다
know where and brought back—I don't know

what.

The King was informed of his return and he
알리다, 통지하다   귀환
ordered Emelian to come to him on the morrow.
명령하다, 지시하다
Emelian again demanded to see the King,
요구하다; 강력히 묻다

219

saying, "I have brought back what I was ordered to; let the King come out to me, or I will go in to him myself."

The King came out.

"Where have you been?" he asked.

Emelian told him.

"That was not the place," he said. "And what have you brought?"

Emelian wanted to show him, but the King would not even look.

"That was not the thing," he said.

"If it is not the thing," Emelian said, "I must break it and let it go to the devil."

Emelian came out of the palace and struck the drum. He had no sooner done so than all the King's troops gathered around him.

They saluted Emelian and waited for his commands. From the window of his palace the King called to the troops, forbidding them to fol-low Emelian, but the troops would not listen to

the King and followed Emelian. When the King
saw this he ordered Emelian's wife to be given
back to him and he begged Emelian to give him
the drum.

"I can't," Emelian said. "I was told to break it
and throw the bits into the river."

Emelian took the drum to the river and the
soldiers followed him. Emelian struck the drum
and broke it into little bits which he threw into
the water and the troops all scattered and dispersed. And Emelian took his wife back home.

From that day the King left off worrying him
and Emelian and his wife lived happily ever after.

🎓 나만의 리뷰 and 명문장